JINGLE MONEY

The Essential Guide to Making Real Money Writing Jingles

WALTER R. DAILEY

Hal Leonard Books
An Imprint of Hal Leonard LLC

Published in 2017 by Hal Leonard Books
An Imprint of Hal Leonard LLC
7777 West Bluemound Road
Milwaukee, WI 53213

Trade Book Division Editorial Offices
33 Plymouth St., Montclair, NJ 07042

Printed in the United States of America
Book design by Kristina Rolander

Library of Congress Cataloging-in-Publication Data

Names: Dailey, Walter R. author.
Title: JingleMoney : the essential guide to making real money writing jingles / Walter R. Dailey.
Other titles: Jingle money
Description: Montclair, NJ : Hal Leonard Books, 2017. | Includes bibliographical references.
Identifiers: LCCN 2017019794 | ISBN 9781495092213 (pbk.)
Subjects: LCSH: Jingles (Advertising songs)--Writing and publishing--Vocational guidance.
Classification: LCC ML3790 .D29 2017 | DDC 781.5/4--dc23
LC record available at https://lccn.loc.gov/2017019794

www.halleonardbooks.com

To Phokeng, my wife,
and Izzy and Christian, my sons.

CONTENTS

PREFACE

Inside you is creativity that you *know* is worth something. However, most of us never fully understand how to convert our God-given talents into something of value. Whether you're just a singer, guitar player, or someone who has great musical ideas, you have what it takes to earn money by making music. Now that you have this book, you have the tools and a path to see real cash by composing jingles.

For some reason, the subject of jingle-making often only appears as a fleeting chapter in a book or is seen in a glimpse within a shallow online article. As a result, the doors remain locked for so many musicians looking to do what I've done—earn hundreds of thousands composing jingles.

A friend of mine inadvertently gave me the idea for writing this book. We were chatting a few weeks ago in my studio when he said, "Walt, I don't know of *anyone* who has made a living off music for as long as you have. That's an accomplishment!" Initially, I brushed off his compliment—feigning humility. But his words sank in; many musicians would kill to do what I've done.

Why should I keep all of this knowledge to myself when someone was kind enough to help me get started? So, I'm paying it forward. This is your invitation to go beyond a cursory overview on the subject. This clear, definitive resource will guide you to do what I've done—earn a lot of money making jingles for businesses!

To your success in music,

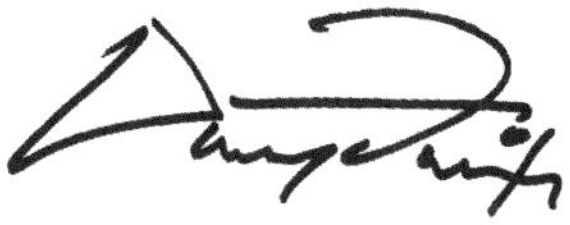

Walter R. Dailey

INTRODUCTION

This book presupposes that you're someone who already knows a thing or two about music. You may be a songwriter, vocalist, instrumentalist, producer, or even someone with a lot of creative ideas. So, as we take this journey, I am not looking to point out where middle C is on the piano or talk about proper picking techniques for the guitar, nor will I discuss such things as breathing methods for singers.

This book is about showing you how to use the musical skill you *already* have, to earn money making jingles.

For many musicians, the concept of making a substantial amount of money is a distant dream—out there with visions of standing onstage in front of thousands, accepting a highly coveted award.

Although I can't give you the steps for becoming the next artist or producer of the year, I most certainly can guide you to a place where you may have previously thought is off-limits—earning cash with your musical talent.

If I can help you earn *hundreds of thousands*, we'd both agree the time and investment you make in this book is well worth it.

Think about it; jingles are everywhere: on radio and TV, on websites, YouTube . . . you name it.

The thing is, there are people, just like you, out there creating jingles for all of these commercials you hear. Guess what? They are getting paid to do something that you most certainly can do!

Despite the money at stake here, I am sure you may already be saying, "I don't wanna be some jingle writer. I'm a real musician!" Well, let's start off with a little dose of reality. I'd like to challenge you, from a dollars-and-cents' standpoint. How much money are you pulling down as a musician? Be honest; it's just you and me here. My guess is, not too much. If you were rolling in the dough, you'd be frolicking on a beach in Maui, jamming out your next chart-topper on a gold-plated ukulele!

Let's begin by checking out the income potential for the average musician out there. The following are a few places you may have considered to make things happen:

- **$.004 on Spotify.** "It's all about streaming, baby!" You've heard that, right? If you managed to get any of your music on streaming services, such as Spotify, I can tell you (at the time this book was written) that you're only getting a fraction of a penny per stream for the song you've spent a wad to record. I've calculated that at Spotify's current payout of $.004, you can afford to buy a latte when your song has reached 1,200 streams! Oh, and if you want an extra shot of espresso, I'd suggest you work your way to a few hundred more streams.

- **$0.99 on iTunes.** Selling music on iTunes is every musician's dream. You're right there with all of the well-known singers and bands. The problem however is, you're right there with all of the well-known singers and bands! The competition is overwhelming and most indie acts are lost in the crowd. When Katy Perry drops a single, she moves a few hundred thousand units in a few days. The rest of us? Well, let's just hope Nana figures out how to download your new single onto to her new phone. Every sale counts, right? When she does, you're going to see a whopping *$0.76*, that is, after Apple takes its cut. Think about this for a moment; you're going to need 150 downloads so that you can afford a halfway decent set of headphones and a burrito. Awesome!
- **$10–$50/hour at your studio.** If you're pretty good with such recording programs as Fruity Loops, GarageBand, or Pro Tools, you can set up your own makeshift recording studio and charge other musicians to record. This can be a great way to make money until you have to fight to get that indie band to realize recording an entire album in one hour is not such a great idea, no matter how much Red Bull they drink.
- **$250–$600 for gigging.** Playing shows around town is a great way to make some cash. But there are a few things to consider. You've got to split your revenue with the band, sound guy, manager, and a gas-guzzling van.
- **$5,000,000 record deal.** Virtually every musician has had dreams of being called into the office of a label exec. The double doors open, he's smiling, and begging you to sign the generous, multi-million-dollar deal. Oh, what the heck, he's gonna toss in the private jet—simply for having interplanetary awesomeness! Record deals are rare these days; deals of this magnitude, even more so. If you're angling to get a big deal, fine. But how do you manage everyday life before landing your contract?!

If you're involved with any of the previous activities, I'm not trying to make you feel like an idiot for doing so. Hey, my music is on iTunes and Spotify, too.

What I'm trying to get you to understand is that, until you finally make it big, you've gotta figure out a way to find some extra cash in the meantime. Look, we've all got daily pressing life-issues, such as taking care of family, paying for studio time, buying gear, touring expenses, or whatever! Why not learn a new way to make money to take care of some of this stuff?

Every time I tell musicians about the type of money they can make in the jingle business, I always notice the same lightbulb go on. "How much can you make?" they ask. After I answer, they'd usually ask one more time just to be sure they heard correctly. Clearly, this response originates somewhere between disbelief and excitement.

Depending on who you write a jingle for, you can make anywhere from *$500* to *five figures* for just *one* jingle! Imagine what your income could be by composing multiple pieces. Now you understand how I've made hundreds of thousands by writing jingles.

It's your turn!

1

TREASURE MAP

Big Mac, Filet-O-Fish, Quarter Pounder, French fries, icy Coke, milkshake, sundaes, and apple pies . . .

—MCDONALD'S

Meow, meow, meow, meow . . .

—MEOW MIX

Like a good neighbor, State Farm is there.

—STATE FARM INSURANCE

Every so often on the news you will hear reports about a random shipwreck somewhere in the ocean, that happened many years ago. Why does it always seem like these types of vessels were carrying some unseemly amount of rare gold coins? If you're like me, you're sitting there, staring at the news report, just wishing someone would give you diving gear and a map to the exact spot where the ship went down. Well, there is a sea, of sorts, out there, and it's called the *Sea of Jingles.* I'm offering you a map and the exact location of the treasure. My hope is that you'll be excited and proactive enough to get off the couch and dive in to bring this treasure to the surface!

Whether it be part-time or full-time, one of the best things about starting your own jingle business, is that it is pretty simple and can be run right out of your bedroom. Your investment in your business can be relatively minimal—a topic we'll cover in detail as we go on.

For some reason, jingle making is one of the most often overlooked opportunities for musicians. And even when people do want to learn how to get into making jingles, no one ever offers clear enough answers. You grabbed this book because you're hoping you'll find something here that will help you do it. Don't worry; I will give you all of the information you'll need to get yourself up and running. In fact, I'll fill you in on a few secrets that no jingle producer has yet to reveal.

Start this journey by knowing you *will* be successful in making money with jingles. But there's a catch. You must fully accept the point of view this guide offers. I say this because I've been to the mountaintop; I have sold many jingles over the past decade. During this time, I've also made a ton of costly mistakes that you can learn from. As I have seen both the good and the bad times in this business, you stand to benefit, as this book aims to eliminate much of the guesswork for you. So, as I pour on the details and begin to tell you stories about some of the things I've done, know that these accounts have purpose. Each and every detail is included to help you in coming up with ideas for your own opportunity to excel in this industry.

The financial and business greats of the world, such as Warren Buffett, Bill Gates, and Oprah Winfrey, are often asked about the keys to their individual success. But have you noticed that their responses are out there for everyone to see? If that's the case, why is it that everyone who hears what these titans have to say about business are not billionaires, too? I'd argue that it comes down to actually *doing* the things they recommend; it's about *execution.*

This guide is no different than the previous example. I will fully uncover clear ways for you to make a lot of cash in this business. However, the question becomes whether you're going to put the advice found in this book to work for you. It's a variable that *you* control.

As we start down the road to learning the jingle business, I will highlight key tips, strategies, and ideas. Some of these concepts will relate to the jingle business, and others will point to entrepreneurship. Some concepts will cover musicianship, whereas others will cover strategy. No matter the idea, know that they all have one common goal in mind—making you a success with music!

The amazing thing about guides like this is that you are able to benefit from *years* of expertise, knowledge, and strategies, after spending just a few hours studying them.

With that, let's move on to your first tip:

Knowledge alone is not power. Action fueled by knowledge is power.

2

WELCOME TO THE SHOW

Virtually every week, I'll get an e-mail or a call from an eager musician, singer, or songwriter looking to sell me a jingle idea for a bit of cash. Typically, I'll hear such things as, "I've got this great idea for a jingle. Do you want to buy it? Are you guys hiring?" My typical answer is no. Am I a conceited jerk not willing to give the little guy a break? No. Whenever a hungry musician calls, looking to sell his music, it tells me one thing—he doesn't know what he's doing! You see, those who've reached out to me fail to realize I'm the *competition*. It's sort of like a Microsoft employee calling up Apple, looking for help with a software problem.

It's time to blaze your own trail. One of the first lessons you need to grasp is do not call up studios and other jingle companies, hoping that they will "throw you a bone"! Odds are, they won't. After all, it's a competitive world out there.

If you're going to send an e-mail or make a phone call, at least point yourself in a direction that is productive—meaning, to someone who actually wants your jingles. I can assure you, calling up would-be rivals is not doing you any favors! In fact, when you drive down dead end streets like this, you stop believing you can ever be successful; it's self-sabotage.

In 2014, it was reported that Beats by Dre was sold to Apple for *billions*. Let that sink in for a minute . . . billions! Do you think this lucrative deal came about because Dre's headphones line was the absolute best product on the market? Nope! The success of this enterprise happened because Dr. Dre and his investors had *business sense*!

If you truly want to make it in this business, I strongly encourage you to take in the business sense outlined here. Being a great songwriter or musician accounts for only a fraction of what you need. So, proactively absorb *all* aspects of this guide. Don't skip ahead in the book, in search of areas you deem *more interesting*. Focus on the boring stuff. People have said, "The devil is in the details." They lied. Truth be told, *the dollars are in the details*! Musicians wind up penniless because they only want to crank out *hot tracks* rather than absorbing the business and strategy side of things—a.k.a., details. These are the same people who call me—just expecting money to materialize because they have musical abilities. I always say, making music is the easy part; it's the business stuff that separates the haves and have-nots.

Dollars are in details, though details are boring.

3

THE BACKSTORY

As for many musicians, the aspirations for music grandeur bit me at a young age. I still recall days in the basement of my parents' house composing one-note songs with my index fingers on an out-of-tune upright piano.

My mother saw no end for my appetite for music, as every Christmas I waged a serious campaign for a shiny new instrument. The first was a tiny Casio keyboard, complete with an 8-bit drum-machine accompaniment and gnome-size keys.

As time went on, my keyboards got more advanced. At this time, MIDI controllers and drum machines were becoming the rage and the cassette tape was the medium of choice.

As I moved into my teen years, I joined a band and became obsessed about music like there was no tomorrow.

It was official. I wanted to be a musician for the rest of my life—making songs and playing on stage. However, as I approached the end of my senior year in high school, I felt the pressure from my parents to choose a *reasonable* career path. As it turned out, I had been pretty good at science throughout school and thought pursuing a college degree in such an area would make sense, from an occupation perspective. Also, I was the first in my family to go after a four-year degree, and the prospect of being a scientist made my dad quite proud. And as if the pressure was not enough, to the amazement of my high school counselors, I got accepted into one of the most prestigious liberal arts institutions in the region; so renowned that it was rumored Chelsea Clinton once had my alma mater on her radar.

To the utter delight of my blue-collar father, I set out to obtain a chemistry degree from the university. As my freshman year came to a close, I realized something: deep in my heart I still had a drive for music. The drive was bigger than daydreaming of playing bongos under a palm tree; I wanted to run a music company, a record label, and explore becoming a writer-producer.

As my freshman year at college drew to a close, my discontentment for a science career grew and so did my courage to tell my father that I wanted to switch my major. In my sophomore year, I sought out a business/marketing major and thoughtfully added music as a minor, fully set on the idea that I would someday run a music company. There is no question; my father was not happy about the revival of the "music thing." However, there comes a time in one's life when one must decide whether to spend time exploring the dreams of others or pursue avenues that fuel personal passions.

Upon completing my degree, I wish I could tell you I jumped off graduation stage in movie-style slow motion, only to land the music career of my dreams. I didn't; far from it, in fact.

When I finished college, I was fully prepared to pursue *the dream*, but reality hit. I was back at my parents' house and dealing with the impending doom of repaying student loans while scratching for some semblance of financial self-sufficiency. My father, now low as ever on patience, was like, "Get a job!" The pressure was so great, I went out and took the first position I could get—a job washing chairs. Yeah, that's right; me and my superpowered degree from the region's hottest school, washing dingy plastic party chairs in a 50-gallon drum of dirty water.

Eventually, I wanted more money and settled on taking a job as an accountant. It just so happened that accounting was the only class in college that I had nearly failed. Imagine dragging yourself out of bed every morning to face something you're not good at *and* hate with a passion! Sound familiar?

During this time, I got married and my first kid was on the way. I began to descend into the abyss of a *9-to-5*; just going to work, deferring the dream. While there is nothing wrong with having a stable job and providing security for yourself and family, there is something inherently wrong with watching your dream die a slow death and doing nothing to resuscitate it.

As I chased more money for my young family, I changed jobs a couple of times and wound up taking a 100 percent commission sales position (which was not the smartest of moves for security). At the time, I heard everyone in this company was making big bucks and I wanted in. After months of sales training, aptitude tests, and rigorous hoop-jumping, I was ready to join the big dogs. I could all but see myself throwing hundred dollar bills in the air, as if in some rap video. The problem, however, came about when I was unable to sell anything. Pressure from my father after college was one thing, but the anxiety and pressure to care for a young family on a 100 percent commission gig was like a good old-fashioned waterboarding. Later, I will explain how my short stint in this position paved the way for success making jingles, though at this time nothing seemed to be working for me.

All of my work frustrations came to a head on one seminal day. That day was September 11, 2001. As you would imagine, the prospect of selling *anything* had all but vanished along with the vibrancy of the US economy. The industry in which I was employed nearly ground to a complete standstill.

A few short months later, I was out of a job—collecting unemployment. Life sucked on a monumental scale. As I eagerly tried to claw my way back into a similar job, I couldn't secure an interview to save my life. It was at this point that I arrived at my what-do-I-have-to-lose moment.

Several years removed from my dream of pursuing music as an occupation, I decided to fire up some music software that I had convinced my wife to allow me to purchase with our tax refund just a year or so earlier. I thought, "Hey I'm pretty good at making beats and music, maybe someone will pay me for it."

Just a few short weeks later, I landed two jingle projects!

Please don't misunderstand; my first paycheck didn't happen magically. Someone with firsthand knowledge on the subject had to, literally, sit down and walk me through the basics.

It's time to write your own story. I'm here to offer you what I got many years ago: a thorough walkthrough on how to make money writing jingles.

Let's do it!

4 KNOW YOUR STUFF

You've seen the infomercials—some sleazy guy on late-night TV—desperately trying to get you to buy some plastic contraption you'll never use. Commercials like these are totally frustrating because they hype up something which appears to have very little substance.

Before getting supereager to sell *anything*, you must first appreciate and know the value of the product you're selling. That's just the beginning; you've also got to be able to get others to see the value in what you're selling—in this case, jingles. When I say *value*, I'm not referring to the price tag on the jingle (although we will get to that later). I am referring to the impact or benefit this musical service can have on the businesses that use them. In many instances, it will be your job to demonstrate to buyers just how powerful jingles can be. In short, you've *gotta know your stuff.*

Just the other day, I was on the phone with a guy who was trying to sell me something. I had a bit of interest in it; however, when I asked detailed questions about the service, he got flustered. When I insisted on answers before buying, he blurted out, "Look, if you want to do business with me, you just have to trust me!" The conversation ended with my walking away from his offer. *Trust him?* No way! The guy couldn't answer basic questions. You won't fare any better with customers if you come off as some slick, clueless-infomercial salesman. There's a lot of money involved with jingles and nobody is willing to risk big money on an uninformed service provider.

So, let's start the process of equipping you with what you need to know.

5

THE BASICS

Before going any further, I don't want to assume that you know what a jingle is. So, let's begin to define our terms:

> *A jingle is a short musical piece, designed to elicit a response, facilitate an emotion, instill an idea, and/or raise the overall profile of an institution, organization, or product.*

The History

Jingles, sometimes known as audio branding, musical slogans, or sonic logos, have served as persuasive marketing tools since the early 1900s. Most believe Wheaties, the breakfast cereal brand, was the first to leverage the power of the jingle way back in 1923.

As broadcast media grew, so did the prevalence of marketing and advertising. As these areas flourished, it brought with it the ever-increasing need for companies to establish distinction for their respective brands.

The media landscape has changed significantly since the first jingle rang out over the airways in the early 1900s. What remains the same is the need for distinction for advertisers—the need to establish recognition, awareness, and trust for a product, service, or institution.

What It's Not

I strongly believe a short musical piece can only be considered a jingle if it includes vocals. In a worst-case scenario, the absence of lyrical content, in my opinion, is just background music. At best, tunes devoid of vocals may be able to be considered theme music.

What's wrong with making background or theme music? There's nothing wrong with it at all. Just know making money from this music product can be quite tough. The odds of a company wanting just *one* of your rock instrumentals may be slim. In an effort to increase the odds, music-only tracks are often compiled into large collections, often referred to as *music libraries*. There are massive companies out there which specialize in this specific aspect of music. They, in essence, are huge curators of music. They thrive on having an overwhelming amount of what some have come to call *needle drop*, *stock*, or *generic music*. If you want to be successful in this area of music, you'd likely need hundreds of well-composed and professional-sounding tracks. You see, success with library music is in *numbers*. The hope is that just one of your top tracks will stand out enough to be incorporated into a huge TV show, movie, or commercial. If that happens, royalties will be heading your way, and in droves. Don't get me wrong; you can sell some of your songs to an established music library company for some quick cash. The downside, however, is that these companies do not pay much per track—maybe $50 to $300 per song. You may be thinking, "Hey, that's not too bad!" But here's the thing: getting your song into an established collection can be very tough due to the amount of competing submissions that come from other musicians. In fact, some libraries have become the newest breed of music industry gatekeepers—to the point you have to be well connected just to have your music *listened* to. It's like dealing with a record label—does the phrase "No unsolicited material allowed" ring a bell? I've heard this enough to know that it's a tough industry to break into.

Acquiring sales from music alone is a tough road to travel in the world of marketing. Shenanigans like this are exactly why jingles are the recommended path.

When first starting out in this business, I was just a guy living in a two-bedroom apartment, composing music tracks with software in a tiny studio. Well, to be truthful, my "studio" was my one-year-old's bedroom. At that time, I didn't really know who'd buy my music. But then it dawned on me one day: what if I called some of the local radio stations? I hear music behind commercials all the time! I thought some of my music tracks could be used in the same way. After a few calls, I finally got a hold of the PD (production director) at the radio station. I began to tell him how my music was the hottest thing since global warming. He didn't really care. Without skipping a beat, he abruptly told me his station signed an agreement which gave them access to, you guessed it, a *music library*. This library was chock-full of music from some of the best composers and studios—a collection of thousands of music tracks. The pieces in this library contained music from all genres: rock, folk, jazz, hip-hop . . . you name it. So, when it came time to getting the right sound for a commercial, the station didn't need to commission someone to compose something original. Those at the station responsible for creating commercials containing music need only to whip out a CD or database and search for the desired style, a process that takes about five minutes.

This story is not meant to discourage you, but instead it's here to help you know what *not* to do. From my experience, calling around and asking radio stations and others to buy *music-only-tracks* has not proven to be a successful strategy for my music career. The primary goal is making money with jingles—not background music. I'm not saying there's no money to be made in writing background music, but that's an entirely different path that requires completely different strategies for success.

If you happen to be a musician without a singing voice, or the other way around, don't worry. We'll tackle how to find vocalists and musicians for your jingle projects later. I just wanted to make the point that the world of jingles, most likely, will demand the lyrical content.

By now you may have the impression that I'm saying the world revolves around jingles. Not necessarily. The reason I am focusing on jingles, to the exclusion of other music-related streams of income, is that jingles are highly lucrative and relatively easy to sell, if you're persistent.

6

WHY JINGLES ARE POWERFUL

Some people think jingles are cute little ditties: something added to commercials when a company has a few extra bucks to burn after dealing with real marketing projects—in essence, an afterthought. Don't get me wrong, I'm sure this has been the case for some. But savvy marketers understand that jingles are some of the most powerful, effective marketing tools ever. While I'll do my best not to bore you with the minutia of mind numbing research, I do think it's important to know why music in advertising is so impactful.

David Huron, author of *Music in Advertising: An Analytic Paradigm*, concluded the following:

> Of the estimated sixty billion broadcast advertising hours encountered by North Americans each year, approximately three-quarters employ music in some manner. Music can serve the overall promotional goals in one or more of several capacities. For the purposes of this essay, six basic ways are identified in which music can contribute to an effective broadcast advertisement: 1) entertainment, 2) structure/continuity, 3) memorability, 4) lyrical language, 5) targeting, and 6) authority establishment.[1]

Let's get a snapshot of what he says about each point:

1. ENTERTAINMENT

> Good music can contribute to the effectiveness of an advertisement, merely by making it more attractive. A good ad engages the attention of an audience, and the most straightforward way of achieving this is to fashion an appeal, which is entertaining.

How fun are commercials? Not very fun at all. In fact, most of us believe the invention of the DVR and its ability to allow us to skip ads may have come down from heaven as an angelic blessing. Why? Enduring commercials, for many of us, is a painstaking experience.

The inclusion of jingles in any commercial takes an otherwise boring encounter and transforms it into an entertaining moment. If you manage to engage an audience with entertaining music, you can leverage the attention captured and, hopefully, sell a product or service. In the end, that's what it's all about in the world of marketing.

2. STRUCTURE/CONTINUITY

> Music may also be employed in various structural roles. Perhaps the most important structural role is in tying together a sequence of visual images and/or a series of dramatic episodes, narrative voice-overs, or a list of product appeals.

There you are, watching a movie, which just so happens to be a thriller. A woman hears an eerie sound emanating in the dark of night. As she tentatively walks down the unlit corridor of her home to confront an unknown presence, dissonant orchestral strings are inserted into the soundtrack—filling each step with tension and apprehension.

Most people aren't even aware of how music is guiding what they are feeling, but it's there—making a significant impact. The use of music in a commercial is no different; if done correctly, a jingle can serve as the framework for enhancing the impact of content observed in a commercial.

3. MEMORABILITY

> Consumers are known to favor products which elicit some degree of recognition or familiarity–even if it is merely the product's name. It is one of the peculiarities of human audition and cognition that music tends to

> linger in the listener's mind. Surprisingly, such musical lingering may occur even when the mind is an unwilling host. Thus, the association of music with the identity of a certain product, may substantially aid product recall.

When my kids were younger, our house was filled with kids' television programming, around the clock. Without exception, the hallmark of every kids' show would be sing-along tunes—designed to teach a lesson. These shows had a song for everything: using the potty, sharing, healthy eating, and the list goes on. Why do you think that is? Why do children first take on learning their ABC's by song? The answer is *mnemonics.* That's just a fancy word for something that helps you to remember information.

For some reason, our brain is wired to retain information that has been couched in a song. If that is true, how powerful would it be for an advertiser or a business to include their name, phone number, website, or product in a song?

A brand can live nearly a lifetime in the mind of a customer by the ingenious use of music.

4. LYRICAL LANGUAGE

> Vocal music permits the conveyance of a verbal message in a non-spoken way. Language utterances can sound much less naive or self-indulgent when couched within a musical phrase rather than simply spoken. An individual can respectably sing things which would sound utterly trite if said. Mixtures of speech and song provide advertisers with opportunities for both logical, factual appeals and emotive, poetic appeals.

When someone speaks, we subconsciously evaluate whether what is being said is trustworthy—truth filtering, if you will. What goes through your mind when the late-night pitchman says, "My product will help you shed twenty pounds in one week . . . guaranteed!" Automatically, our psychological defenses go up; skepticism is placed on high alert. That's because the logical parts of our brain begins to deduce whether the claim seems to be plausible: "'Twenty pounds . . . one week' . . . Nope. This guy is definitely a con artist."

Singing, on the other hand, is unique in that it is one of the few forms of communication which lures the audience into participation, *regardless* of what is being said. We've all caught ourselves singing along to something, only to stop midway and say, "Whoa, I didn't know those were the lyrics!"

All of this time, the words were there, but somehow they managed to elude the logical part of your brain. That is why, for example, it is advisable that advertisers sing, "We're number one!" as opposed to saying it.

Vocals are unparalleled in delivering the message—any message.

5. TARGETING

> Musical styles have long been identified with various social and demographic groups. Musical style might therefore assist in targeting a specific market. The style may function as a socioeconomic identifier—a device for addressing a specific audience.

When a club-bangin', four-to-the-floor EDM (electronic dance music) track makes an appearance in a commercial, chances are my father is not going to sit at the edge of his seat with bated breath. On the contrary, he's likely to change the channel. Why? He's not the intended *target* of the advertiser.

By selecting a certain genre of music, marketers can go after a very specific segment of the audience—all at the speed of sound. There's no need for an announcer to say, for instance, "Hey there, young kids between the ages of eighteen and twenty-four, check out our snazzy clothes! Look cool when you hang out with your friends!" Besides, having an announcer do something as ridiculous as this only highlights the fact that there is a sales pitch in progress (run, kids!).

Using music as an auto-audience-selection tool allows the advertiser to go directly after the group it seeks—without being weird or awkward. This practice serves to strengthen marketing efforts, as communications to customers are done with laser precision.

6. AUTHORITY ESTABLISHMENT

> Closely related to the targeting function is the use of music to enhance an ad's credibility, to establish its authority. Indeed, it may be the case that effective targeting is merely the result of proper authority establishment.

Perception is reality is an overused (yet true) phrase that my former sales trainer used regularly. An expertly styled jingle can make a business look and sound like a million bucks. Imagine listening to your favorite radio station, only to hear the cleverest and most professional, indie-folk jingle ever. After the commercial is over, the simple yet infectious melody stays with you for hours. What prestigious brand could be behind such a masterful sound? Odds are, you'd be surprised if this captivating sound was drafted to advertise Hank's, the Sleazy Pawn Store Emporium, right? The point of this illustration is to prove that the right jingle can bring about a certain level of panache and credibility to a product or brand—even if not warranted. Perception is everything. If done correctly, your music can elevate your customer's profile.

The Power of Emotion

We've seen this perplexing story a thousand times; a man wanders down to the car lot in search of a trusty sedan or minivan to transport his 2.5 kids to school and their various sporting activities. While at the dealership, something catches his eye: a two-seat, seven-speed, 450-horsepower machine-of-awesomeness. Oh, did I mention it's a drop top? Given the gentleman's finite budget and immediate transportation priorities, this sculpted roadster shouldn't be anywhere near the realm of possibility. But, you know what? He takes a test drive. He asks the salesman about all of the features and options. He glares at the sticker price—trying to see whether there is any conceivable way to make this whole thing work.

This is a classic example of logic versus emotion—reason versus the heart.

Emotion, feelings, and the heart are much stronger predictors of behavior than reason. In fact, a lot of our emotions are at odds, or even in a death-match with the rational side of us. Over the years, multiple studies have concluded that emotions usually win the majority of these internal battles.

It has been reported that 70 percent of purchasing decisions are fueled by emotion, whereas the remaining 30 percent of what we opt to buy is predicated on reason.

If you were to advise your client on how to set up a brilliant marketing campaign, what would be the best piece of advice you could offer to get customers to act? You'd recommend a marketing campaign that goes straight for the heartstrings, not the mind.

Emotion-driven marketing is the absolute most powerful form of persuasion there is.

Noted consumer psychologist Peter Noel Murray, PhD, uncovered even more compelling evidence on the matter of emotions and buying behavior:

- fMRI neuro-imagery shows that when evaluating brands, consumers primarily use emotions (personal feelings and experiences) rather than information (brand attributes, features, and facts).
- Advertising research reveals that emotional response to an ad has far greater influence on a consumer's reported intent to buy a product than does the ad's content—by a factor of 3-to-1 for television commercials and 2-to-1 for print ads.
- Research conducted by the Advertising Research Foundation concluded that the emotion of "likeability" is the measure most predictive of whether an advertisement will increase a brand's sales.
- Studies show that positive emotions toward a brand have far greater influence on consumer loyalty than trust and other judgments which are based on a brand's attributes.[2]

So, how does all of this mushy, emotional stuff come into play with jingles? The answer is pretty straightforward: music drives the heart, unlike anything else.

Author Malini Mohana presents the following case in *Music & How It Impacts Your Brain, Emotions*:

> Music is a common phenomenon that crosses all borders of nationality, race, and culture. A tool for arousing emotions and feelings, music is far more powerful than language. An increased interest in how the brain processes musical emotion can be attributed to the way in which it is described as a "language of emotion" across cultures. Be it within films, live orchestras, concerts or a simple home stereo, music can be so evocative and overwhelming that it can only be described as standing halfway between thought and phenomenon.[3]

There's a lot more research that can be brought to bear on the subject of music in marketing. But, as I said before, I do not wish to overwhelm you with a ton of facts. However, you should know, without a doubt, that jingles are effective.

In wrapping up this chapter, we can say, without hesitation, that music drives emotions—emotions dictate behavior—behavior pushes the buying decision—a buying decision creates revenue.

Maybe now you can see why there is money to be made in composing jingles. Businesses are established to create revenue. Your jingles can literally help businesses make money!

Never forget that what you create has real value.

7

RECORDING THE PERFECT JINGLE

Okay, we've covered jingle history, research, and some foundational info.

However, if you don't have a clue as to how to make a solid jingle, we've wasted our time. So, that will be the next order of business.

Allow me to interject a bit of advice before going any further. *Being a brilliant songwriter does not automatically make for a great jingle writer.* Being a virtuoso or amazing vocalist does not necessarily mean your jingles will be sought after. Success in creating jingles for businesses will require a unique combination of things—a delicate mixture of art and science.

The creation of jingles is a very challenging proposition for many musicians—even me. I say this because composing music for commercials is all about getting the world of marketing to overlap with the world of musicianship—the old Venn diagram scenario. As you start down this road, you may get the sense that you're dumbing down your craft or that you are not truly striving for the outer edges of creativity. This, my friend, comes with the territory.

I recall working on a jingle project for a dentist. When I was done creating the first draft for the practice, I felt incredibly satisfied with my creative efforts. I'm being modest; it's more accurate to say that I felt that my jingle would be fast-tracked to win an advertising award for hottest jingle in the world, and maybe even this quadrant of the Milky Way! But let's not move too quickly on the accolades. My practice speech for my award was summarily killed after I got feedback from my client. The dentist was dumbfounded; the client heard *no* genius in my, self-dubbed, audible awesomeness. In fact, the dental practice proceeded to systematically rip my music to shreds with one "we don't like this" comment after another.

The moral of this story is simple: *your* view of creativity isn't everything in this business. Develop a thick skin and make a mental allowance for the possibility that *creativity* may be shifted to the back burner, in exchange for a humdrum, highly predictable—yet effective—melody.

Let's delve deeper into this.

Good or Bad: Who Cares?

With the exception of dealing with national/international brands, I wouldn't obsess too much about how good your jingle sounds. No, the previous statement is not a mistake. Whether your jingle is hot or horrible, know that there are much more important issues you need to be concerned with. So, before throwing this book away, give me an opportunity to explain the logic behind my earlier statement. You see, music is quite subjective. What may sound great to me, may sound terrible to you and vice versa.

If you think about it, differences on what sounds good play out just about everywhere. For example, certain groups of people feel rap music is noise—absolute cacophony. Some feel that hip-hop is one of the most important means of expression in modern-day music. Who's right? Well, no one, technically. But whatever answer just popped into your head proves the point—you have an opinion; you are biased. And just as you can vehemently argue your side, someone else can do the opposite.

As you create jingles, you will eventually create a piece so inspiring, you'll ask the Grammys to create a new category—just for your jingle. You, of course, would win that year—with such brilliant writing, and all. Meanwhile, back in Realville, your client will inform you that your jingle has completely missed the creative mark—in short, it sucks.

The point of all of this is to get you to understand one simple thing: your job is to create a sound your client likes. That's it. Supersimple. After all, that's who is footing the bill for your service. This is not to suggest that you can't dialogue with a customer about how to make the jingle sound better; I'm saying that if you get to a place where the customer digs in its heels about a desired sound . . . comply. As you acquiesce, do it without pouting or making the other party seem like abject idiots for disagreeing with you.

With the subject of creativity decidedly put to rest, let's talk about the science of creating the perfect jingle. For all of you free-spirited musicians out there, please don't cringe at the word *science*. Know that the creation of a really good, solid jingle is quite formulaic. If you think about it, just about *all* music you listen to these days is formula-based. Whether it be country, pop, urban, or rock, you're going to hear the following: *verse, chorus, verse, chorus, bridge, chorus*. Boom. I've just summarized 95 percent of all songs on the radio, Pandora, and iTunes. So, when I speak of composing jingles in a systematic way, just accept that it's the musical world we live in.

With that said, let's identify the building blocks for the perfect jingle. As you implement each, you're all but guaranteed to nail the perfect jingle—*every time*:

- Company name
- Infectious melody
- 5-second rule
- Perfect timing
- Targeting
- Structure
- Soundcheck

Company Name

Earlier in the book, I established the fact that music will etch itself into our mind—destined to live in our memory indefinitely. Yeah, it's a heavy concept, but that's simply how our brain is wired.

As a kid growing up in the '80s, I was really into the European group Art of Noise. I thought these guys were absolutely brilliant composers (still do). Recently, I heard one of their songs on the radio, and, just like that, I was instantly transported back to my childhood. "Man, it's been years!" I thought. As I listened, I recalled epic break-dance battles in the driveway of my friend's house, hanging out until the streetlights came on, and trying to squeeze the last drops of fun out of the waning summer vacation in late August. Don't worry, I won't drag you any further down my memory lane. I injected this story because most likely you've had a similar musical experience—a song that takes you back in time. Your mind is instantly filled with song lyrics you haven't thought about in years!

What does nostalgia have to do with inserting the *company name* and making the perfect jingle? When you produce a jingle, you are creating music, which, by default, will create memories. If your jingle is crammed full of meaningless lyrics, guess what? People will file these meaningless words away in their memory. If, on the other hand, your jingle contains the *name of the company or product*, you're assured to etch that name into the mind of the audience forever. The apex or chief goal of all marketing is *name recognition*.

With that in mind, there's a real possibility that you may be thinking that I've just stated the obvious. But you'd be wrong—really wrong.

I've observed countless jingle producers on a local and national scale omit the name of their client. These jingle makers have inexplicably opted to use some type of tagline or other generic phrasing—to the exclusion of the name of the company or product!

Recently, I heard a jingle for a local heating and air-conditioning company. I have to admit, the sound of the jingle made me a little envious. Its production value was off the charts—it sounded amazing! The vocalist and the instrumentation sounded like it was put together in a high-end L.A. studio. However, the name of the HVAC company was conspicuously absent from the jingle. The jingle writers chose to use these words instead: "Turn on the air. Turn on the air . . ." They threw in a few other words, too, but never one line about the name of the business. They gave that critical responsibility to the announcer . . . a bad choice.

As outlined before, a catchy tune will stay in your mind, playing over and over. Having the *name* of your client on repeat in somebody's head is far more valuable than having a nebulous catchphrase occupying that space. After all, what's the point of a catch phrase if you can't place where it's from?

We are exposed to several thousand advertising messages on a daily basis. Think about that—*thousands*! Ads are changing every six seconds on digital billboards. They are wedged into your favorite apps. Marketing messages are plastered on the backs of sales receipts, and the list goes on. If, in this highly saturated environment, you are able to pull the *name* of your client out of obscurity and make it a fixture in the mind, you have won a significant battle on behalf of your customer. You've conquered the onslaught of thousands of competitive messages. This victory is courtesy of simply adding the name of your client into the jingle.

Infectious Melody

At the heart of any musical hit or captivating tune is a memorable melody.

Should you not be well versed in the technical aspects of music, let me crudely define a melody as the most recognizable lines in a song that you can either sing or whistle along with.

As you build the melody or the main singing part of your jingle, it is important to make it supersimple. As a creative person, it may irk you to go with a plain Jane, vanilla melody that seems irritatingly pedestrian. Deal with these restrictive feelings and know that now is not the time to exchange a simple melody for an atonal experiment with didgeridoo and distortion.

For you to have true success in crafting a great jingle melody line, I'd like to offer the following suggestions:

- Use repetitive words.
- Use repetitive note patterns.
- Use repetitive rhythm patterns.

These concepts would even be powerful as individual strategies; however, were you to somehow fuse them all together, you'd be a veritable musical genius. Does the idea sound overwhelming? It shouldn't. In fact, I'll go a step further and state that it's an incredibly simple exercise. Look no further than your favorite childhood songs for proof: you got it—nursery rhymes!

You'd be correct in thinking that nursery rhymes are fun, toddler-friendly tunes, fit for kids just learning the alphabet or counting. But it goes deeper than that. These tunes live in the mind for a lifetime. That's because the pillars I outlined earlier are present. This musical structure creates an unshakable memory—etched in the psyche forever!

Let's examine one. We'll use "Twinkle, Twinkle Little Star":

WORD REPETITION

The first line in the song kind of makes my point. The word *twinkle* is used in succession. This type of repetition all but guarantees that you will remember some of the words—namely, *twinkle* in this example.

NOTE PATTERNS

The word *twinkle* has two syllables (twin-kle). The writer of this tune assigns both the first and second syllable of this word with the same note. So, were we to perform this song in the key of C, you'd play two Cs for the word *twinkle*. Then two Gs, two As, and so on. With the exception of a few words, this simple melody is comprised of a series of "twos." (See the following illustration.)

RHYTHM

Finally, the rhythm for the melody (the timing of the notes, for the less technical folks) is pretty much the same throughout. If you are versed in music theory, understand that a succession of quarter-notes account for most of the rhythm, the words *star* and *are* being the exception in the version depicted. Sure, this rhythm pattern is quite elementary—lacking cool syncopation. But its simplicity makes it easy to remember, easy to sing along with. And in the jingle world, that's invaluable.

The next time you're composing a jingle for a pizza joint or furniture store, put your melody up against an old nursery rhyme. You may discover ways of making your composition even stronger.

5-Second Rule

This piece of advice has nothing to do with how much time you're given before you're legally banned from eating that yummy fry you dropped on the floor.

The 5-second rule goes back to what I mentioned before. We are exposed to thousands—maybe even tens of thousands—of ads a day. This reality has trained all of us to have a shorter attention span.

Think about it: why was Twitter thought to be so revolutionary? It simply managed to restrict the *length* of communication down to manageable, fun-size chunks: in essence, get to the point and then . . . get out of my face!

If you want to be highly successful at making jingles, it is imperative that you *grab the listener in the first five seconds*. Avoid protracted musical intros, instrument solos, or even throwaway lyrics at the beginning of your jingle. Get right to the point in five seconds or less! Failing to do so may result in people changing to a different station, turning off the ad your jingle is featured in, or engaging in other media, such as smartphone use, while the ad is playing. If people are tuning out your jingles, how can you convince a company to pay thousands for a product that's *not* being heard?

Combine all three tips mentioned thus far: jump right in by singing the name of your company, pair it with the memorable melody formula, and captivate your audience immediately. When you do this, you are giving the company you're working for a fighting chance at being remembered once the ad is over.

Perfect Timing

Another critical building block for jingle writing success is timing. When I say *timing*, I'm referring to the actual length of the jingle you write.

For the most part, you're likely to compose jingles for radio, TV, and cable commercials. One of the inherent restrictions in these places is time. The majority of commercials will last anywhere from five seconds to two minutes in total length. Here's a breakdown on commercial lengths:

2:00 infomercials, pharmaceuticals, public service announcements
1:00 radio ads, infomercials
0:30 TV, cable, and radio commercials
0:15 TV, cable, and radio commercials
0:05 radio commercials

Of course, there will be exceptions to what I have outlined; however, just know that these times are widely accepted.

When beginning to produce a jingle for a client, you must be keenly aware of these times, as your composition will be dictated by the length of the commercial. You cannot go a fraction of a second beyond the allotted time for the medium on which your jingle airs. In fact, most broadcasters use software that automatically prepares the string of commercials that we see and hear. This software operates with absolute precision and will not allow one commercial to be 31 seconds and another 29 seconds. What does that mean for you? Your music must start and end within the prescribed time frame while sounding natural and complete.

So, before recording your first note, you need to know the length of the ad. When you do, strictly adhere to the time you're given.

With that in mind, let's get a little technical. If the following goes over your head, get someone who records with a DAW (digital audio workstation) and/or someone who knows about music theory to help you out.

When I start to compose a jingle, one of the first things I do is look at where my tempo/beats per minute (bpm) is set in my software. Is the lightbulb coming on yet? If you don't know where I'm going, let's explore this further. The bpm for your project will inform how much you're able to do, musically, within your larger time frame. For instance, if you set your recording project's bpm to 100, you can fit 25 bars/measures into a 1-minute jingle, assuming that the time signature is 4/4. In fact, I'd highly recommend composing the vast majority of jingles in this meter, since in Western music the 4/4 time signature is widely used and accepted. Music constructed with multiples of 4s feels very familiar to virtually everyone in your audience—hence its other name, *common-time*. In the end, your jingle should come out to be about 24 bars (4 beats/measure x 6 measures). That means you'll wind up with a jingle that's about 2.4 seconds shy of the 1-minute mark. I use the remaining seconds to allow the track to come to a close with something such as a slight delay (echo) or reverb, placed on the last note of the jingle. From there, I fade the residual sound down as the piece approaches the absolute cutoff point. Understand that going over the time allowed, even by a half-second, will result in calls for retakes, stating that the jingle has to be adjusted—no exceptions. Don't put yourself through the hassle. Work out your project times *before* starting!

One more note about timing. I used 100 bpm as an arbitrary tempo; feel free to use whatever tempo you want. As you do, keep this fact in mind: the slower your tempo, the longer it will take to sing words. If your vocalist is spending too much time just getting the lyrics out, it can encroach on the announcer's time or other commercial content.

We can examine how tempo affects vocal timing by going back to our nursery rhyme for an illustration. Let's say we begin a 30-second jingle with the phrase *twinkle, twinkle little star*. In doing so, we'd be using 2 bars, or 8 beats. If the tempo is set to 80 bpm, it will take a singer 6 seconds to get these words out, leaving 24 seconds for other commercial content. Now, let's say we speed things up and make the tempo 120 bpm. It will only take a singer 4 seconds to sing the same words—a 33 percent improvement! This change leaves 26 seconds in the commercial. One or two seconds may not seem like a big deal, but I can tell you that when an advertiser is only given a moment to get people to buy a product, every single second counts. As someone creating jingles, you must know and respect this seemingly small little window of time.

Targeting

We touched on this earlier: targeting is the deliberate act of reaching out to certain people, a particular segment of the audience, what most in the marketing world call *demo* (short for demographic).

Targeting is basically when a commercial is communicating, "Hey you! We're talking to you!" without actually saying, "Hey, you . . ."

Imagine a commercial that begins with a sequence of shots depicting a silver-haired couple in their late sixties strolling across the beach. Do you think a twelve-year-old watching the ad will be on the edge of his seat, identifying with the lifestyle shown? Not likely. If, however, the viewer is married and nearing retirement age, the ad may be more appealing. Advertisements are designed to resonate with you. As you watch, you may start to see yourself in one of the characters in the commercial. Or you may aspire to be like one of the characters shown. Whatever the case, know that you've just been targeted.

Music is one of the most precise targeting tools there is. As a result, your job as a jingle producer is to use its power to help your client reach the right people. If your client sells toys, you're most likely to target kids and moms with your compositions. Hence, your musical ideas will take you to sounds that will appeal to them. If you're working for a luxury car dealer, chances are you won't be inserting any kazoo tracks into the jingle; instead, you will be looking to create a refined, upscale sound.

I recall working on a jingle for an RV dealer who is located in the South. At first, I thought this would be a pretty easy project, as I'd had great success with a previous RV dealer who happened to be located in Nova Scotia. As I began to send draft ideas to the southern dealer, things quickly started to head in the wrong direction. Okay, things were going south (sorry, I couldn't resist the pun). I thought the sound was great, but it was not what was wanted. Finally, the owner told me that the jingle needed to be a country jingle—not rock, jazz, or modern anything—just old-school country! I knew I'd be able to write a country jingle. But wait—the client got even more specific: "I want it to sound like something from George Strait." As I went through this painstaking process with my client, I learned that country music was everything to the dealer's audience. This genre of music went well beyond his personal preferences; it was indicative of a particular lifestyle—a lifestyle the RV dealer was selling. By using country music as the backdrop for the jingle, we were able to appeal to a very specific segment of the population rather quickly.

In short, use a music style or genre as a device to draw the right people to you.

Structure

As you are well aware, the average jingle isn't really long—just a handful of seconds. Despite the limited time frame, it is important to create subdivisions or sections within this tiny space. There are two reasons why this process is very important: *musical interest* and *cuts* (also known as edits).

Let's get into each of these things.

MUSICAL INTEREST

Repetition in the jingle world is a good thing; however, too much repetition can start to undo what you're looking to accomplish. To preserve *musical interest*, I highly recommend breaking up the monotony with a brief change in chord progression, melody, or words. To make what I'm suggesting clearer, let me suggest that you view jingles as miniature songs. Songs, as you know, don't drone on and on with the same four bars; they have sections: verses, choruses, bridges, and so on.

If you're hired to draft a jingle that is to last the entire length of a commercial (more on this later), I recommend using what I call the *ABA method*. By the way, this is not an attempt to steal any thunder from a Swedish musical act. With the ABA method, each letter represents a section of the jingle. Section A will contain one or two of the following: the company name, product name, slogan, phone number, web address . . . in other words, the stuff that has to be remembered. Section B is to contain supporting details. You know, "fluff"—ancillary company info that is not mission critical.

Let's take a look at the words from a jingle I wrote for Glacier Dental:

Glacier Dental, nothing says confidence like a great smile
Glacier Dental, nothing says confidence like a great smile
A healthy smile is waiting for you
We'll make you feel comfortable . . . that's great news

Glacier Dental, nothing says confidence like a great smile
Glacier Dental, nothing says confidence like a great smile

Can you pick out the ABA method? The first two (repeated) lines are Section A, the second two lines represent Section B, and then we're back to the initial words to finish things up. Now, you may be getting tripped up over the number of lines being used. Don't focus on that. This method is about offering guidance for major changes (or lack thereof) in your jingle.

The previously mentioned example only deals with word changes. Remember, there are other changes you can make which will promote distinction for your ABA setup. In addition to lyrical changes, you should strongly consider changing up the chords, melody, and possibly the rhythmic patterns.

Before moving on, let me state that the ABA method is not something that you have to hold fast to. I've composed jingles with a number of patterns. Some started with a Section A. Some started with an announcer and then came Section B and then A. Other jingles only had a Section A at the very end of the commercial. The point is, there are numerous patterns, some of which your client will tell you to make. And while you may not have the liberty to explore the ABA method, in its purest form, I feel it is one of the most effective jingle patterns. With the A sections appearing twice, you can establish mind-etching repetition. The B section provides a break and allows for space for supporting content.

Now that I've introduced these variables, it's a good time to talk about the next important topic: cuts.

CUTS

When you begin to sell your jingles, businesses that know a thing or two about this marketing tool will inquire about *cuts* (also known as edits). These two terms refer to possible variations of the jingle. When I say *variations*, I'm not talking about converting a jazz jingle into a rock-themed jingle. These variations primarily deal with length and vocal content and are typically based on one musical theme. So, when my clients ask me about the type of cuts they will get with their purchase, they are asking me how many versions of the *same* jingle they will eventually receive for their investment.

Allow me to give you a couple of examples to bring this concept into focus.

Imagine your client wants to air two completely different commercials to promote a credit union, and wants the jingle to be featured in both ads. Each commercial will be 30 seconds long. The first commercial will contain a series of shots showing customers smiling and making transactions. As a result, the credit union wants the jingle and singing to last a full 30 seconds. The second commercial, however, will feature the credit union president talking about the merits of doing business with his institution. For this ad, jingle lyrics need only to appear in the final 10 seconds of the ad. In this example, the varying jingle lengths represent two different cuts.

Cuts are designed to deal with a number of variables that commercial content can pose. For example, there are ads that feature customers talking. Some ads have announcers. Other ads have spokespeople, and the list goes on and on. As a jingle producer, you will be called upon to make vocal content fit around these instances. Each time you move singing tracks around in your composition, you are creating—you guessed it—cuts.

Let me go over the different types of cuts there are. As I go through these, know that the descriptors I assign to each may change, depending on who you speak with. However, I will use the terms that are most widely recognized throughout the industry.

FULL-SING

A full-sing cut is when the jingle is designed to occupy the entire length of the ad. During this time, vocal content will be present. If the commercial is to last 30 seconds, a "full-sing-30" (a term used by many in broadcasting), this version of the jingle has singing for this *entire* time. If the jingle is to be used in a 60-second ad, vocal content would have to last for—you guessed it—a full minute. Typically, full-sing jingles *do not* any leave space for announcers, voice-overs, or testimonials. This version of a jingle, by the way, is where you'd use the ABA method (outlined earlier).

SING-OUT

In a sing-out cut, vocal content appears at the very end of the commercial. This cut often presupposes the music you created is playing throughout the entire ad in the background, just like a music bed.

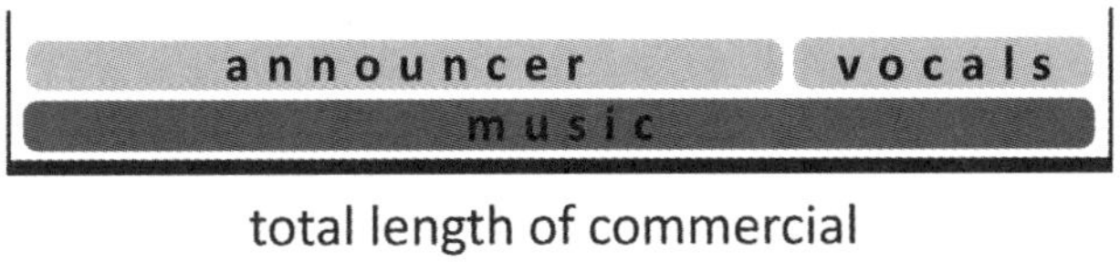

SING-IN

A sing-in cut begins with vocals and then scales down to your music track only. This leaves the remaining time open for other commercial content.

DONUT

A donut cut requires that you remove vocals from the middle of your jingle. This open space in the middle will be reserved for announcers, testimonials, and so on. A donut will provide singing in the beginning and at the very end—vocal bookends, if you will. As with the previously mentioned edits, know that your music should be playing throughout.

STINGERS

Unlike the other cuts mentioned, a stinger does *not* involve music playing throughout the ad. On the contrary, stingers, by definition, are very short. This particular cut should last anywhere from 3 to 7 seconds—tops. Stingers are great choices for tiny ad spaces, such as those ranging from 5 to 15 seconds. Also, stingers can be dropped into longer commercials where music beds aren't needed.

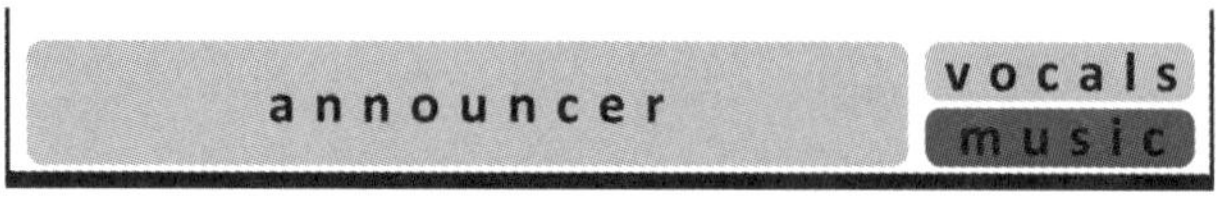

total length of commercial

As you read on, we'll cover how the number of cuts or edits you provide affects how you structure your jingle contract and the price you charge. As a result, you should know that your clients—or those making commercials on behalf of your clients—will be asking about the types of cuts you provide. Get familiar with the terminology beforehand so that you sound like a pro when discussing your services.

8

NO COPYING!

We can't have a discussion about music creation and not address copyrights. As we get into some of the legal stuff, know that *I'm not a lawyer*, nor am I'm looking to replace advice you should be getting from your attorney—a fact that I'll remind you of as we move along. With that being said, I want to touch on this legal topic, as it will affect how you create and protect what you produce.

I'm fully aware of the fact that the subject of copyrights can literally fill an entire book, so I won't attempt to distill the enormity of this topic into this section. I will, however, point out a few things you should know with respect to the jingle business. Here are the areas I'd like to address:

- Inspiration
- Your rights
- Parodies

Before jumping headlong into these areas, let's quickly talk about what a copyright is.

Knowing Your Copyrights

First of all, the term that we're talking about is a copy*right*, not copy*write*. I'm emphasizing this distinction because I've observed musicians using the wrong version of this word. "What's the big deal?" you say. Well, using the word *copywrite* (which is wrong) may lead you to use variations of this word—variations such as *copywritten* and *copywrote* (neither of which are real words, by the way). Using these made-up words will, firstly, make you sound like a person who doesn't have the slightest handle on grammar. Second, it will be a telltale sign to those in the biz that you're a pretender, not the real deal. If you've used this word like this before, don't feel bad; just suck it up, move on, and start using the correct term.

So, what is a copyright? In the United States and many other countries, a copyright is a *right*—a protected entitlement afforded by your respective country.

When you make any sort of original creative work and place it on something—we'll call this "medium"—you (and only you), have the legal *right to copy* what you've created. A medium can be a sheet of paper or a computer, a smartphone or a CD, cloud storage or your bedroom wall, and the list goes on. So, if I were to jot down song lyrics on a napkin at a local coffee shop, those words are automatically protected, or *copyrighted*, according to US law. You actually don't have to fill out some kind of official form or register anything to possess a copyright for something *you* created. But wait a minute—you've probably heard otherwise, right? Well, there is a process whereby you can officially register your creative work with the US Library of Congress and obtain documentation verifying your copyright. This step is highly recommended, as it becomes easier for you to defend your creative work in court, should you ever get into a legal battle over your creative property should it appear that someone else is laying claim to or using it without your permission. However, whether you register or not, you possess the legal right to copy your own work. It's up to you to decide if you want to formally slap a padlock on your music by sending it into the Copyright Office in Washington, DC. But for the sake of not deviating too far, you can research this topic on your own by going to www.copyright.gov.

One more thing about copyrights: you are *not* afforded copyright protection for a creative thought floating around in your head or tunes you create in the shower. Again, you'd have to get it onto some sort of fixed medium first, such as lyrics written on paper or audio recording on your smart device.

Now that we've got a better picture on what a copyright is, let's get back to our topics.

INSPIRATION

If you're pretty new to the jingle game, it would make a lot of sense for you to listen to other jingles out there as part of your education. Pay attention to what sticks with you; make notes about what you hear to help you with your recordings. As you go through this process, be sure to adhere to this simple advice: *do not blatantly copy another jingle or song.* Why? Well, as we just covered, you do not have the *right* to copy someone else's work. I'm emphasizing this because I've met people and musicians who go beyond inspiration and delve into copyright infringement. It's one thing for you to fill up your smartphone or computer with songs you should've paid for (which is wrong, by the way); it's an entirely different matter when you steal another jingle maker's music and present it as if it is your own. Thievery like this—airing the stolen jingle concept to several thousand people, with the name of your client's business attached to it, is a sure way to be sued into oblivion.

I once had the owner of a construction company ask me to create a jingle for his business. The problem, however, is that he wanted to use a really popular rock song from the '80s as the theme for his jingle. I told him I could make something similar to it, something with the same feel (though the lawsuit brought against Pharrell Williams's take on Marvin Gaye's style makes me nervous about mimicking "feel"). No, he insisted, he wanted to use the exact song, with a minor tweak to fit in his company name. I then told him that we'd have to obtain the rights from the song's publisher and writer for doing so, but he didn't want to pay the huge fees. He just wanted to blindly use the song. I warned him in the most direct and clear way that copyright litigation isn't anything to toy with. He casually insisted that he'd deal with the consequences if they were to ever darken his doorstep. Yep, he was an idiot. Understand that this guy ran a multimillion-dollar construction company. What do you think would happen if word got back to the record label, publisher, writer, or artists that their superpopular song was being *copied* and they weren't getting a penny for it? He would be a prime legal target, especially as he looked to smear the sound of his illegal jingle across every radio station in the city!

I share this story because you should never be cavalier about copyright infringement—whether it's you stealing someone's work or a client asking you to do it for them. The risks are way too high.

It's okay to get ideas from others; however, it's not okay to drag-and-drop full concepts from others.

YOUR RIGHTS

At the beginning of the section, I mentioned that a copyright automatically gives *you*, the composer, a right to copy your own creation. What happens when your client wants to copy *your* work? This is kind of like a trick question. The whole reason that you grabbed this book was to ultimately do just that: get a paying customer to copy your work—share your music with the world by airing it on TV, radio, or distributing via the web.

I raised the initial question to make a nuanced point. Your client has the rights to copy your work *only* if you give them permission to do so. When you agree to record a jingle for an advertiser, that's implied. However, you should take the proactive step and *detail your customer's allowance to use your material for advertising in the contract/agreement* you sign with this client. I'm taking the time to emphasize this point because it is *your* work we are talking about here. As the copyright holder, you can opt to restrict *how* someone uses your material.

As an example, I always charge companies less money if they are going to use the jingle I created in one small city. I tell them (in writing) that they are limited to the geographic area we agreed upon. If they were to grow into a huge company—beyond the limits we discussed, and wanted to air my jingle everywhere, they'd have to pay more money for me to allow *my work* to be copied in such a fashion.

I exercise my rights as a creator so as to protect my interests. I would totally be ripping *myself* off if I allowed work I created for one tiny town to be used on a national scale without seeing commensurate compensation.

This is the same rationale for laws against software piracy. It absolutely sucks for a software company to spend countless dollars and coding hours on an app, only to have one guy buy the program, proceed to share it on the web and have others download the application a billion times—all without any further money going back to the developer. This translates to more use and less pay. What if somebody did that to you and your music? Let's say a song you wrote reaches one million downloads, but you only got a total of 99 cents from iTunes. Oops . . . make that 76 cents (remember: Apple needs its cut). You would be enraged!

I don't mean to make this a moral soapbox, but hopefully you'll start to have newfound respect for the sanctity of creative work, especially if it were work you were hoping to make money on.

In summary, know your rights and the rights of other creators; there's money to be made . . . or lost, for that matter.

PARODIES

I purposefully saved the topic of parodies for last. I wanted to establish a basic understanding of copyrights before tackling this area.

If you're not aware, a parody is simply a humorous rendition of an original work—think Weird Al Yankovic (Google him, if you don't know).

I bring the subject of parodies up because they are used a lot in the jingle world, mainly because they are funny. As I'm sure you've seen with ads that appear on Championship Sunday—football's biggest day—"funny" is always a winner.

So, let's get back to the subject at hand. With the expectation of poking a little fun at original work, can you make a *copy* of copyrighted work without getting into legal trouble? Wouldn't that be seen as infringement if done without obtaining the rights to do so? Not necessarily. As I mentioned earlier, the subject of copyrights is a pretty extensive and complicated topic. I'll go as far as to say that there are a lot of gray areas.

If you do your homework (and you should) on the laws, you'll come across the term *fair use*. To make things simple, you could say that fair use is a legal allowance that gives you the ability to copy copyrighted material for the expressed purpose of critiquing, referencing, or, in our case, parodying an original work. In many instances, this can be done without obtaining permission from the author, writer, or creator of the material being used. In the United States, fair use follows the spirit of *freedom of speech*—giving one the ability to cite, talk about, or make jokes about creative work which has protections.

This concept, for instance, allows movie critics to show a short clip of a film, with the intent to rip it to shreds in a review, if merited. It gives the newscaster the ability to read off words from a book about zombies that teenagers are going crazy about. It gives a blogger the ability to quote research findings from an article.

So if you're ever asked to make a parody jingle for your client, you're in the clear, right? Hold on just for one moment; there are a few things that factor into whether fair use is allowed—four, to be exact.

1. Purpose: Are you copying the work for commercial or noncommercial purposes? Is the copy you made *transformative*—will your work be seen as something totally new or different?
2. Nature of Copyrighted Work: Are you borrowing from published or unpublished work?
3. Amount Used: Are you copying the entire work or borrowing the core parts of the work?

4. Devaluation of Original Work: Will the replication of the work negatively affect the market value of the work?[1]

Do each of these factors raise questions for you? Are they confusing? Well, I've been at this for a while and I can tell you I still find these points confusing. So, here's my advice: *avoid making parodies for your clients*. There are too many variables involved in determining whether you're in the clear to do so.

Nothing will crush your growth faster than dealing with legal matters that are over your head. In fact, there are even major disagreements among legal professionals regarding the rules of the road, as it relates to copyright law. Why go down a path that even the best and brightest have a tough time navigating? Stick with the stuff you know. Your life will be a lot easier!

Soundcheck

Testing 1-2, 1-2 . . .

Now that your jingle is just about done, you're going to need to check your levels.

As I get into this section, there's a chance that I may introduce terms or concepts that you're not totally familiar with. It may be because you rely on someone else to help you with the technical aspects of recording or because you are still in the learning stages and have yet to come across things I'll cover. Whatever the case, I will not venture too far into the science of techniques presented, but we have to stick our toe in the water. Besides, this book isn't meant to be an exposé of audio engineering—that would leave us juggling quite a bit of info. So, take it upon yourself to do further research if you find your eyes glazing over while going through this section.

Earlier, I mentioned that choice of music style is a pretty subjective topic. Someone may call a tune great; another person may declare it to be total crap. Let's just leave it there. What I want to do is move beyond personal hang-ups and move to universal truths, as it relates to the audio quality for jingles. So, if you feel your brain combating the following advice, don't chalk it up to individual preference. Know that the following will help preserve your reputation as a recording professional in this niche industry.

VOLUME

Let's deal with one of the most obvious indicators of your work quality—volume.

In the marketing world, one has to use any and all angles to stand out in the crowded world of commercials. Loudness happens to be a major one. Have you ever noticed how commercials seem to be crazy loud as compared to the show you were watching or listening to? Spoiler alert: it's done on purpose. As the commercial break arrives, marketers have to grab you by the throat, or I should say ears, before you wander off. Although it can be jarring, high volume is often used to seize the attention of the audience. You may not like contributing to such madness, however, that's the business you're looking to get into: a world of out-competing the neighboring commercial, by any means necessary!

With this understanding as a backdrop, I strongly suggest that you *normalize* the final version of your jingle audio file. In other words, adjust your overall volume so that it tops out at 0 dB. If, on the other hand, your meters (the green bars indicating volume) on your master fader (main volume knob) are going red, you are most likely *clipping*, or exceeded the noise level for your software; that's too loud. As a result, you run the risk of sending clients slightly distorted audio.

Personally, I throw a brick wall limiter into my master bus (last in the chain, of course), to guarantee that I take my sound right to the edge, but no further.

DYNAMICS

Next, let's tackle dynamics—meaning, the loudest and quietest points in your recording.

If you pay close attention to audio changes in commercials, you'll realize that volume for music and jingles are lowered just as the announcer, actors, or voice-over appears. Unless asked, *do not create a jingle that goes up and down in volume* to achieve this effect. The creation of a commercial tends to have many participants, one of which will be a video or an audio editor. Their job will involve moving the volume of your jingle around commercial content. For this reason, you should maintain a relatively consistent volume level throughout your jingle.

To achieve a full and consistent sound, locate your master bus and insert a compression plugin. Try using a ratio of 8:1, with a threshold between –6 dB and 0 dB, and the knee set to 9 dB, to smooth over any major spikes in volume. Follow this with a brick wall limiter.

A final word about dynamics: Do not use a wide dynamic range for style purposes. In other words, do not allow the track to go from a low volume to high, or vice versa. If you were drafting a film score for Hollywood—big highs and subtle lows—this approach would be right on the money. But we're not making music for a summer blockbuster here. This is the commercial world; the overall volume should be consistent. You've got just a few precious seconds to make your case with your jingle. Don't waste them by experimenting with orchestral dynamics. If you do, chances are some of your audio will be . . . well, inaudible.

NO "PAN" HANDLING

When producing music for artists, I'm a raving fan of LCR panning. The LCR technique usually means that vocals and instrumentation will be panned hard left, hard right, or straight center. In my opinion, this method adds great depth of sound to the listening experience. Whether you like LCR panning or prefer to pan your tracks somewhere in between, know that panning of any type may come back to bite you when producing jingles.

Allow me to explain via a personal experience.

I once created a jingle for a tourist destination in Orlando. I was pretty satisfied with the final sound. My recording featured a supersoulful female vocalist and these punchy horn blasts that echoed from far left, to right, and faded out while bouncing back and forth. So as not to step on lyrical content, I carefully positioned the horns in between the vocals where there were rests (pauses) in the melody. I also set the delay on the horns to match the project's tempo, to provide a deliberate rhythmic edge in the music. After completing the jingle, I sent all of the audio files to the commercial editor. After a few weeks of them shooting footage and editing, I was sent a copy of the final commercial. Upon listening to it, I felt as though something was off; my jingle sounded horrible. It was weak and awkward. Apparently, the editor wasn't a big audiophile, and when he had imported the music into his software, he had converted the track into *mono*! Even worse, he didn't smash my left and right channels into one. No—he only imported the left channel of my audio. As a result, my horn blast repetitions were halved and other panned instruments were weaker and/or missing altogether. When this jingle left my studio, it rocked. When hearing it stripped down like this, it sounded anemic and underwhelming. All of my thoughtful panning was for naught.

With the previous story in mind, I'd caution you to keep the vital contents of your jingle somewhere near the middle. This is not to suggest that you can't record in stereo or that all editors or commercial producers will strip off one channel. I'm simply trying to get you to understand the risks of going too wide.

One more note about panning. There are times when the medium will mandate a single channel for audio. AM radio is a prime example. If your client airs your jingle on the AM dial, know that you're not going to have the benefit of stereo sound—just one channel. The same would be true for a jingle that is to be used for an on-hold phone message. Furthermore, if your jingle is to be used or heard on a mobile platform, know that many smartphones will play back your jingle with only *one speaker*.

> After completing a stereo recording, switch your master bus output to mono and observe the overall quality and integrity of your jingle. Make adjustments until the mono version of your recording has all of the necessary parts.

MIXING

Should the kick be louder than the bass guitar? How do you EQ an acoustic guitar so that it does not muddy the piano track? I don't want to dive into these types of mixing questions. Go do your own research if these types of questions are burning in your mind. Instead, I want to talk about the mix you establish between your music and main vocals.

As an indie music producer, I often seek to place my artists' vocal tracks right in the music mix—not too loud, but just slightly under the overall music mix. However, when I put my jingle producer hat on, I have to depart from this mentality . . . and so do you.

After doing this for so many years, I've learned that lead and melody vocal content should sit *on top* of your music—not in it. I say this because many of your customers will demand it. Plus, your job is to make the vocal content stick with the audience. For that to happen, the clarity of the lyrics cannot be obscured by instrumentation.

The other day, my wife and I were talking about a song we both know. As we talked about the song, I recited some of the lyrics. The record-scratch moment came when she turned to me and said, "Those aren't the words." Really? All of this time, I've been singing the wrong thing? I'm sure you can identify with this mishap.

If you're not careful, you could end up having people doing the same thing with the jingle you create. To safeguard against such an occurrence, get your vocal mix out front so that people can sing along and remember the *correct* lyrical content.

9

ALL SYSTEMS GO!

Now that you've got some solid info under your belt, you're probably very eager to get things going. So, let's get into setting up your jingle business.

In the coming chapters, I'm going to go through things that you *must* have and things you *should* have.

Please note: if you are missing something from the "Must-Haves" chapter, I will offer up recommendations as to how to get these items quickly and/or easily. So, if you come across something you're missing, don't assume that your jingle business will never get off the ground. Just know that we may have to do a few things to make sure the right pieces are in place. Again, I will walk through those pieces to ensure that you have what you need.

As for the "Should-Haves" chapter, know that items listed will aid in quick growth and will serve you well when dealing with competitive forces. But again, don't feel the absence of these items means you are unable to start.

I learned a long time ago, *the best thing you can do to make money is to simply start.* Even if you make a few mistakes along the way (I'm hoping with my advice, mistakes will be few), just get in the habit of *acting.* This is a mind-set that will place you far ahead of most musicians out there.

10 MUST-HAVES

To get things off the ground, you're going to need a basic framework for your business. This framework will give your efforts substance and stability. Invariably, you're going to come up against some type of resistance, challenge, or obstacle. So that you don't give up at the first sign of uncertainty, you will need some key things. Here are the must-haves for your business:

- Come up with a business name.
- Create examples/demo.
- Develop a jingle contract.
- Establish payment acceptance.
- Plan for Uncle Sam.
- Create a business structure.
- Secure a talent pool.

Business Name

This may seem obvious, but it's very important to put a name to your business. The assignment of a name establishes validity both for you and potential customers.

Imagine a mother giving birth to a baby and deciding that "human" will suffice as a way to identify the newborn. This scenario may seem a bit ridiculous (unless you're an eccentric New Age hipster, looking to defy the norm), but it underlines the fact that names are a vital, yet basic, way to establish importance and distinction. So, assigning your jingle production company with a name is highly recommended. As you think about names for your jingle business, be sure to vet any of your name ideas with Google. You don't want to find yourself battling with another jingle producer who happens to be using a similar if not the same, name. No matter how creative your moniker is, do yourself a favor and check around first. You'll save yourself the headache later.

Let's get back to name choices.

Choose a name that is somewhere between cool and familiar. More specifically, try combining an offbeat name with the word *jingles* or *music*.

For instance, let's use the name "Rocket Fuel Jingles." My made-up name engenders something cool while still telling you what it is.

Also, when choosing a name, be sure spelling does not become an issue. Let's go back to the Rocket Fuel Jingles example. Let's say you're feeling your creative mojo and decide to spell the name of your business as, "Rokit Phule Jinglez." What will be the potential impact on your business? Chances are people will never be able to find you, on . . . let's say it together . . . Google. Why? You've made your name so complicated that people will never type it right on a search engine. Although it should be obvious, I'll run the risk of saying it: having a business that can be easily found on a search engine is a massive deal.

The issue of name choice can cut both ways. Let's look at the opposite side of creative names. Let's explore pedestrian, vanilla, boring names.

Say you decide on a name like "The Jingle Company." What are the odds this name will help you stand out? It won't! It's too generic. People will have just as hard a time finding you on the web with this name—given the vast number of results that will most likely appear on a search engine.

Beyond this, common or bland names are simply forgettable. If it were me, I'd want my name to grab people and elicit a response!

If you're unsure, jot down your top five name choices and ask the opinion of others you trust. Once the frontrunner has been identified, create a list of four completely new names and add your previous winner to the new list, for a total of five. From there, ask around again. You can repeat this pattern for as long as you like until you wind up with a name that resonates with others and is absolutely perfect.

How to find a name

- Use your first or last name.
- Borrow words from other easily recognizable languages. For example, something in Spanish/French/Italian could probably be recognizable, whereas something in Turkish might not be.
- Blend two words or two names together.
- Create a name which has recognizable components, e.g., "Soundamax."
- Use fun, quirky random words, e.g., "Habanero Jingles."

Examples/Demo

When I started my jingle company years ago, I'd call around asking any- and everyone whether they wanted a jingle. I made, what felt like, a billion random calls to anyone who would listen. Looking back, it probably wasn't the best strategy (by the way, we'll get into where to make calls in just a while). Every so often the odds were in my favor when making calls and I'd happen across someone who expressed interest in my jingle services. As it turned out, I wasn't really ready for somebody to actually give me a shot. When asked about samples of my work, I didn't have much to offer. Remember, I was just getting started. As I struggled for a solution to this quandary, I decided to piece together samples of my best music tracks. I'd hoped the interested party would see just how impressive my composition skills were. Then reality hit. The potential client didn't care to hear these samples because they were all music-only tracks and stuff for indie artists—nothing related to commercials.

This type of scenario is always frustrating for people just getting started. It reminds me of that age-old experience conundrum: You see a job posting somewhere in which experience is required; you're thinking,

"How can I get experience if no one will give me a chance to get experience?" Everyone's asked this question at least once in his or her life, right?

In the world of jingles, this scenario plagues musicians all of the time. When you get started, I guarantee you an interested buyer will eventually ask for a sample or reel of your music.

For the uninitiated, a "reel" harkens back to the days where actors would, literally, bring in film reel to audition for a certain role. The reel displayed clips of them in action. Over the years, a reel (or "demo reel") has come to be the go-to phrase for those in the media or entertainment industries. In essence, your reel is a sample of your work.

So, back to what to do when you *don't* have a reel. The simple answer to this problem is: *Make one up*!

When I was getting my start, a company in town had expressed interest in buying a jingle from me. Sure enough, it wanted to hear a sample of my work. After some thought, I'd decided to make up a fictional company to be featured in the jingle. The name of the faux business in my jingle was "ABC Company" . . . no kidding!

As I got started on my jingle demo, I knew very well my vocals wouldn't cut it. I've never been anything close to being a singer, so I got a friend from college to drop by my studio/apartment/second-bedroom to record some tracks for me. The recording came out pretty sweet. It sounded like an actual commercial . . . kinda surprised myself!

After I was done editing the sample with my recording software, I was ready to send it over. Here's the thing: I didn't want to misrepresent my recording—trying to make the client believe ABC Company was a real business that I'd worked with. So, what did I do? I simply told the business that the jingle was an *example* of my capabilities—that's it. All this potential client was concerned with was whether I could do the job. And my jingle reel proved it, without any doubt.

This encounter resulted with my signing two contracts with this company. I wound up making about $3,000 on the deal.

At the time, I had no stable income. And, boy, I can tell you, bringing in this type of cash for a few hours of work, on my own schedule, felt tremendous!

The point I'm looking to make is that even when you're just getting started and have no client list to put on your résumé, you're still going to need strong examples of your capabilities. Nothing will demonstrate this clearer than an actual jingle—though it may be a made-up jingle. Now, before you slam this book down and run off to score your first jingle reel, know that creating your sample will require some know-how. Skip back to "Recording the Perfect Jingle" and build from there. As you do, embrace the idea that an essential building block of your jingle business will be having something relevant for people to hear.

Jingle Contract

The other day, a friend of mine was recounting an event our group of friends attended a few years back. As he told the story, I couldn't help but feel that his recollection was a bit off. As the trip down memory lane continued, we began to debate all of the details surrounding the get-together so many years before. Our debate over the facts was friendly but pointed. The participants in the conversation insisted that their version of events was the right account of what had transpired. Hopefully, you understand where I'm going with this.

Contracts are necessary because people simply forget things, not necessarily because someone is out to cheat you.

Imagine arguing with a client over how much money it owes you. Imagine debating with a customer who is demanding services or extras that you never agreed to provide. I have a philosophy: contracts never matter until real money and time are involved. When dollars and cents are at stake, you will find exchanges between people can sometimes get a little chippy, if not downright heated if someone feels he or she are not getting what was promised. As a guy or gal running your own business, you really should have a sense of structure and process, and you need to have agreements put in writing. The last thing you want to do is put yourself in a position where you are fighting with a client. To avoid such tension, I encourage you to take the time to create a contract whereby all of your terms and parameters are clearly spelled out for everyone to see. Only set out to work when you have a signed contract.

Now, you may be thinking, "Well, of course working *without* a contract is stupid." Before you gallop away on your high horse, I can tell you there may be times when the idea of a signed contract is the furthest thing from your mind. How could this happen? The funny thing about this business is that when the prospect of money shows up at your door, the excitement is so great; it's tough to think about anything other than getting right to earning the pile of cash staring you in the face. If your rent is due, for example, you may not be thinking, “Hey, let’s slow this thing down and think about this sensibly.” All you want to do at that moment is find out how fast you can get some money from the deal and if you’ll be paid in cash (not a good business practice, by the way). The realities of pressing, personal financial obligations can very easily mitigate any common sense you have.

To make sure that the excitement of hastily doing a deal does not come back to bite you down the road, do yourself a favor and make it a point to draft a jingle contract now. Go a step further and turn it into a template so that you can use it any number of times, as needed.

If the words “I’m not a lawyer and can’t afford one!” are dancing through your head right now, I get it, but please don’t let the idea of creating a contract deflate you. Getting a contract set up for your clients is not as hard as you think. There are tons of sample contracts online to borrow from for inspiration. I will also provide you with a sample contract in “The Contract” chapter so that you’ll have something to go from.

Once you’ve located a sample contract, it is advisable to reach out to an attorney for a review of what you’ve found.

One more note about getting a lawyer: If you can, seek out the advice of an entertainment attorney, preferably someone who’s worked on the music side of things. Simply because someone has been anointed to practice law in your state doesn’t necessarily mean he or she knows anything about drafting jingle agreements. Just as there are many types of doctors out there, pediatricians, proctologists, and so forth, attorneys also have areas of expertise. Some of them specialize in patent law, some lawyers will clean you out in divorce proceedings, and others will knock you over in hot pursuit of an ambulance. Although many types of lawyers will have a basic understanding of contracts, those who work in the areas of music and entertainment will have a much greater grasp on what matters most to those working in this business—such issues as copyright law, licensing agreements, royalty negotiations, and so on.

Let’s get into a few key areas your jingle contract should cover:

- Services provided
- Payment terms
- License terms
- Clauses for handling problems

SERVICES PROVIDED

Your contract should be very detailed and specific when it comes to what you're agreeing to provide. Don't feel pressured to write out a fifty-page document detailing every nuance. But a few clear sentences should do the trick.

Your contract should cover: the length of the jingle, the number of cuts that will be included, the amount of lyrical content that will be included, an outline of content contributors—the number of singers, types of instruments to be used, and so on.

PAYMENT TERMS

How, when, and what you're going to be paid is pretty important stuff, right? Be sure your contract clearly states these terms. Later, I'll get into what the typical agreement consists of. But for now, just know that your terms, whatever they happen to be, must not be ambiguous.

Your contract should include the following: when payment is due and how you're to receive money (check, credit card, PayPal).

OWNERSHIP TERMS

As a working musician, you've got to have a handle on who will ultimately own the music you create. Typically, when a business is seeking out a jingle, you're going to find yourself on one of two roads: the one-time fee or work-for-hire path. There's also licensing—all of which we'll dig further into as we go along.

Over the years, I've had a lot of businesses that wanted me to sell all of my creative rights, along with the purchase of their jingle. In other words, they wanted to own the jingle I created, outright. In the music world, this is known as *work-for-hire*—being paid for your efforts while surrendering ownership of something you've had a direct hand in creating.

The other road is a one-time fee (also covered in more detail later). This way presupposes that you retain your rights in what you create. As a result, you can dictate how long, how often, when, where and what your music can be used for. There are a myriad of options for one-time fees, some of which we'll explore in the "What to Charge" chapter. For now, understand that should you retain partial or full rights to a piece. The terms of your music should be crystal clear, lest you find yourself battling a business over something *you* created.

Hopefully, you're now seeing the importance of what we covered in the "No Copying" chapter.

CLAUSES FOR HANDLING PROBLEMS

As you've gone through the previous points, you've probably started to recognize that things can veer off the road you're hoping to travel. Don't start sweating bullets; that's the point of a contract, right? I alluded to the fact that we all sometimes lose sight of where we're headed and a contract is the perfect tool to keep everyone on track. So, never view a jingle contract as a one-sided tool of devilry—a legal means of jamming someone in the eye. No, a contract should be a mirror of a reasonable agreement made between two parties, whereby each side receives benefit.

It is my experience that the addressing of potential problems in a contract actually prevents them. For instance, if I include a clause that tells the client that it will be charged an absorbent fee for paying late, chances are, it won't pay late! If it doesn't agree with such terms, guess what? It won't sign your agreement in the first place. That may suck for you, but at least you'll know you're dealing with a client who may have hang-ups about paying on time.

Payment Acceptance

If you're looking to be paid in nonsequential, unmarked bills, maybe you should guest star as a bad guy in an action movie. As stated earlier, don't think for a minute getting paid in cash is a good business practice in the jingle world. Don't get me wrong; I fully understand that cash feels easier—there's no waiting for checks to clear, no credit card transaction fees . . . I get it. Maybe you're used to getting paid cash from street performances or gigging on the weekend, but just know that this world is totally different. The first difference is the dollar amount. As I've been saying throughout this book, you stand to make thousands with *each* jingle transaction. Your clients aren't carrying around this type cash in their back pocket, I can assure you.

It's funny—the one and only client I ever had who paid me in cash literally had his assets seized by the feds and the IRS, after it was discovered he and his business partner had bilked investors out of millions. At the time, it felt kind of weird getting paid in crisp $100 bills. But, hey, I could leave my client's office and head right to the gas station, hit the grocery store, and buy fast food for the kids on the way home—talk about convenience!

The problem with getting paid cash in general is that the paper trail is very loosey-goosey. It makes for poor accounting. Whether it be on the client's side or on yours, proper financial records are a sign of a stable process.

So, what ever happened to my cash-paying client? His name was plastered all over the newspapers due to shady financial practices. I'm not saying this is true of all business owners who pay in cash. I am saying it's a red flag.

BUSINESS BANKING

One of the first things I'd recommend for you as a jingle business owner is to set up a proper business banking account. As you would imagine, I recommend opening up this account using your official business name. While financial institutions have varying rules about setting up accounts, it is important to do your homework to find one that will help you get things started fairly easily.

When I first got started, some banks required business certifications, documents, and articles of incorporation. At the time, that seemed a bit too complicated; they wanted things I did not have. After doing a bit more research, I came across a bank which only required the standard identification and federal tax ID number. As it turned out, obtaining this ID number wasn't so complicated. I simply filled out a few forms, made the government aware of my business name, and that was it. After a short amount of time, I received my tax ID. This is also known as EIN (employer identification number). I made my way over to the bank and, after filling out a boatload of paperwork, I had an official business checking account. From that point on, I was able to start collecting checks in the name of my business.

CHECKS

Let's talk about the most common way of accepting payment in business—receiving checks. Only moments ago, I alluded to the idea that your business should be set up at the bank. As you start your business, you invariably will come across the question "Who should I make the check out to?" Don't wait until this time arrives to start fumbling for an answer. In your haste, you may be tempted to have checks made out to you. From my experience, having people write checks out to you personally is not professional at all. You may disagree with me on this, but what I can say with confidence is that appearance in business is everything. If you appear to be a fly-by-night, flimsy operation—taking checks as an individual rather than an institution, may threaten your credibility. People have more confidence, in most instances, when dealing with a structured business rather than with a guy looking to make a quick buck. Hence, if you do not have a business name (as discussed earlier) and a banking system, I believe you will fall into the latter category—just someone holding a "will work for food" sign.

CREDIT CARDS

Next, I'd like to get into the acceptance of credit card payments.

When working with some smaller businesses over the years, I've been asked about whether I'd accept a credit card payment. You see, many businesses you'll encounter fund their operations with credit cards—a pretty common practice. I've even had business owners tell me they were seeking more reward points by using their cards for purchases. In either case, you may be asked to accept this type of payment and it is incumbent upon you to be ready for such a request now, not later.

There are tons of ways for you to set yourself up to accept credit cards through institutions such as: PayPal, Google Wallet, Square, and the list goes on. Many credit card processors will not charge you any money to set up an account, which sounds awesome, right? Not really. The reality of using such companies is that they take a small percentage of your revenue. Typically, you can expect to have about 3 percent skimmed off the top of your earnings. If you're thinking, "Hey, that's not so bad," I'd like to remind you of the type of dollars we're talking about here. Remember: in the world of jingles, the price tags are pretty big. That means your credit card fees will also be higher, should you decide to accept plastic. Let's say you agree to sell a business a jingle for $3,000 and the client wishes to pay via card. The card processor will take approximately $87 from you. This is enough money to tackle a small bill or cash for a fun night out.

I am not bringing up the fee issue to discourage you from taking credit cards; I simply want you to know the realities of commerce. I don't like credit card fees, but understand it's often a necessary part of doing business. So, why would I recommend something that I'm not that fond of? There may come a time when accepting credit cards may be your only option. Also, there may be an instance where the convenience of doing so outweighs all other options.

For example, I once worked on an international project. The client was based in another country. This customer insisted on sending checks. There was a massive delay in waiting for the delivery of the checks. Once payment arrived, I had to wait even longer for the bank to cash the check, given exchange rates and clearing funds from an institution out of the country. In this instance, getting my hands on my cash took weeks. A credit card payment would have been better.

If you can wait, opt for a check. If you need your bucks sooner than later, you may decide to bite the plastic bullet.

TRADE ME

Before closing out this section on payment, I'd like to mention one more way to get paid: in cookies! Okay, maybe you'd prefer something else. Let me clarify.

A good business partner of mine has used *trade* as his means of payment over the years. Although I've never been real big on trade, he's managed to make it work quite well. He's negotiated furniture, vehicles, new carpet for his house, equipment, and advertising services . . . you name it. I cannot independently verify that he's ever negotiated cookies, but I've gotta believe it's happened.

If you decide to go down the trade road, I'd like to offer a word of caution. Be sure your trade suggestion matches the value of service provided. For example, if you are creating a jingle for a home builder, do not ask them to build a 4,000-square-foot home in exchange for a jingle. The suggestion is preposterous and will most likely damage your credibility. Ask to swap your services for something of similar value. Refer to the "What to Charge" chapter for guidance on the worth of your jingle.

Don't Anger Your Uncle

It's time to deal with your unruly family member . . . Uncle Sam.

Oh, don't play coy. Everyone knows good ole Uncle Sammy! He's the planet-size wet blanket at the party who comes to squeeze a few coins out of your pockets. If you haven't caught on, I'm talking about paying taxes.

Earlier, I told you I'm not a lawyer. Newsflash: I'm not a financial planner, either. With that firmly established, I've got a colossal piece of advice for you—*pay your taxes*!

Oftentimes, businesses I've worked with have asked me to fill out W-9 forms before sending payment for a recording project. These W-9 forms are a way for companies to substantiate investment into their respective businesses to the IRS. In other words, they can write off a certain portion of advertising expenditures come tax time. Here's the thing: when your W-9 form is collected, it triggers MISC-1099 income for you that year. In other words, the IRS knows you're out there and how much you've put in your pocket. As a result, it'll track you down faster than Liam Neeson if you haven't paid your fair share. When Uncle Sammy finds you . . . he *will* kill you . . . figuratively, of course. The point is Sammy has the nose of a bloodhound and he'll detect your earnings miles away.

Just do the right thing from the start.

I recall having a banner year writing jingles. We're talking six-figure income. Jealous? Don't be. Shortly after the year ended, I recall filing my taxes and thinking, "No, that can't be right!" As it turned out, I was on my way to paying the largest tax bill ever! It was virtually as much as somebody with an average income could earn in a year! Sure, I was able to write off some business expenses, but they weren't nearly enough to break the kung fu grip of my star-spangled aggressor . . . Uncle Sammy. I won't get into a long story about this, but all I can tell you is that my lack of diligence in dealing with my taxes put my business behind for *years*! I should have immediately set aside money for taxes, with every transaction.

I want to be sure the education this book offers is not based purely on sunshine and puppies. I hope that my sharing some of my boneheaded choices, such as tax stupidity, can help you bypass a lot of heartache.

So, allow me to say it one more time: Pay your taxes!

When the dough starts rolling in, get the help of a tax professional. It'll be worth it. And besides, if you're paying taxes, you're making money—glass half-full, my friend!

Business Structure

Whether you're making jingles part-time or full-time, your business needs backbone. What I'm really saying is your jingle company should operate under a structure that will protect your interests.

If you can, set up your business as a *limited liability company*, also known as an LLC, or Ltd.

When you give your business such a structure, you begin to take certain risks and legal liability off of your shoulders, from a personal standpoint. For instance, if your business were sued and your accuser won, there are certain protections that may prevent your personal assets from being seized—assets such as your house, car, or your prized '80s-style gold rope chain.

Procedures for setting up a limited liability company varies from state to state. Do a bit of homework on the process in your area and take steps toward protecting your interests. Don't wait until someone threatens everything you've worked for. Do it now.

Talent Pool

This may be an obvious one, but you're going to need some musical content to offer customers. If you happen to be a versatile musician—able to sing, play, and edit—you may not see this as a big deal. Despite your abilities, you're going to need a deep talent pool to help you as you grow your jingle business. If you're someone who lacks one of the core skills (singing, playing, or recording), it will be especially important for you to have a reliable talent pool.

I've always been quite proficient in scoring the genres of R&B, hip-hop, and dance. As it turns out, I've probably produced far more country-based jingles than anything else throughout my career. I've been asked to replicate the sound of modern country, old-school country and western, Garth Brooks to George Strait—you name it. In the beginning, I developed twangy, fake renditions of what I felt country music was. I quickly began to offend my clients—those who really knew the genre well. As a result, I began to seek out performers who were proficient in this particular style of music. They'd walk me through various melody structures, appropriate harmonies, enunciation, chord progressions, instrumentation, and more. Eventually, my clients were completely dazzled. My jingle company now had the capacity to replicate a sound that resonated with a particular audience—all courtesy to finding a few people who were capable country singers and loved the music themselves.

With that little tidbit in mind, start networking with a variety of singers, instrumentalists, music editors, and producers to deepen your talent pool. You don't have to make any commitments to these people now. All you are doing is starting a conversation with other musicians. In fact, this will be a conversation most are happy to have when they understand you may potentially call on them in the future to collaborate and *pay* them for their expertise.

Get out there now and find a few people. Oh, and saying, "I don't know other musicians," is not an excuse, but a reason. There are plenty of ways to start building a network.

One of the easiest places to find musicians and other music professionals is your local music store. Just walk in the front door and you'll hear artists all over the store playing a ton of licks on the various instruments. Strike up a conversation and invite these people to stay in touch with you. It's just that easy!

When you are out gigging or enjoying a live show at a local venue, reach out to the musicians there. Chances are, they are just like you, looking for additional opportunities. Most likely, they'd be happy to speak to you about connecting on a potential jingle project.

As a guy who has been involved in a church community most of my life, I can tell you that some of the best musicians I ever come across are guys who are there every Sunday morning playing for the choir. Making an appearance at church may do you some good, and networking with these talented musicians may do your business some good as well.

Building your talent pool can even be as easy as searching the web for local people. There are a ton of networking, classified boards, and interest groups you can look up to find people. Given the technology we all have access to, these people do not have to live in the same city! If you need a hand with a project, you could easily have people work remotely for your project. Have them record vocals, tracks, or guitar licks for you and upload them to the cloud. Once they're done, just drop their audio into your favorite digital audio workstation (more on that in a moment).

I once hired a guy out of the Middle East to lay down a few vocal tracks for one of my clients in Alaska; I did all of this from my studio in Ohio. My singer would send back his raw vocal tracks and I would edit and mix them and subsequently fire off the completed piece to my client in the Northwest . . . supereasy.

I've gone through the same process with vocalists in Nashville and L.A. This has always looked great for my company—telling clients that I have hired session vocalists from these music meccas. Clients, in turn, feel as though their projects are getting the absolute best creative treatment ever.

There are a number of ways to find people all over the world who can participate in your project: ReverbNation, Twitter, voice-over sites, Bandcamp, Craigslist, music job boards, and the list can go on for days. Just do your homework.

Finally, whoever you work with, be sure to *pay* them. Set the terms and conditions in advance of any work. Never have people do work for you at no cost unless you are auditioning them or demoing your service to prove your capabilities to a client. I have a strong belief that if you are being paid for something, people working with you should also be paid. Later, in the "Hiring Other Musicians" chapter, I'll discuss how much they should be compensated.

11

SHOULD-HAVES

Now I want to get into a few areas that will give you an edge over your peers in the business. If you have OCD tendencies, try to remember the next few pointers are things you *should* have, not *must* have. So, resist the urge to "get all your ducks in a row" before getting started. Just get started. As you grow, layer in the following:

- Recording software/DAW (digital audio workstation)
- Business phone line
- Website
- References
- Brochure

Recording Software

As I thought about recording software, I initially wanted to make it a must-have item. However, the more I pondered it, the more I believe having recording software is strongly recommended but not imperative. I say this because if you have someone in your talent pool (as discussed earlier) who can record and edit for you, this area is no longer an impasse. I would like to make clear, however, that having recording software will most likely save you lots of money in the future, as this area can be one of the most time-consuming aspects of jingle creation. If you resign yourself to paying someone else to do this for you, keep in mind that such participation will potentially eat into your profits. I assume most of you know what recording software or a digital audio workstation (DAW) is, but again, I don't want to leave anything to chance. A DAW is used to record and edit studio-quality audio and instrumentation via a desktop computer, laptop, or even mobile device (such as a tablet or smartphone).

As you consider purchasing recording software, I realize there are scores of programs out there to choose from. A few brand names come to mind: Pro Tools, Sonar, FL Studio, Ableton, Cubase, and a host of others. Just read a few reviews and buy the program that best suits your computer, laptop, or tablet and your level of recording needs.

There are a number of benefits associated with digital recording: unparalleled sound clarity, limitless multitracking (the ability to record and combine a number of instruments and voices), ease in sharing digital files with off-site collaborators, nonlinear editing, nondestructible editing (preserving original recordings while applying various filters and effects), and the list goes on.

After purchasing a DAW, spending an afternoon reviewing online tutorials for your specific software may save you thousands of dollars over the long run. The more you can understand and do with your program will benefit you greatly.

With the right finesse, you can achieve a sound which rivals the pros out there.

In fact, the overwhelming majority of major multimillion-dollar studios in Los Angeles, New York, and Nashville use the same software I outlined earlier. To be frank, I've heard of huge studios that keep massive soundboards perched in front of a recording booth to appear that they are the best in the world. Truth be told, they'd all turn out the same sound . . . *without* the 50-foot-long mixer.

It's all about *how* you use what you have. If you have a good enough ear, you could break out an old-school 4-track and totally rock a jingle (I'm showing my age with this example, I know).

The point is, purchase and become proficient with the basics of a DAW and you can work recording wonders.

Business Phone Line

I recently reached out to a lady by phone for a business transaction. When the caller picked up, it wasn't the woman I was trying to reach; it was her jealous boyfriend. By the tone in his voice, you could tell this person was highly suspicious of my call, and yeah, you would be right to assume this person was quite unprofessional—thinking I was some sort of threat to his personal relationship.

What would happen if a big client called you? Would your kids, grandma, or a psycho-jealous partner going to answer your phone? What about you? How would you answer if you did not know a client was calling?

For some reason, a few people out there have a habit of sounding like idiots when answering calls. And guess what? Nothing will kill a promising deal faster than having a client call you and get that type of first impression experience.

Your solution: *a dedicated phone.*

If all you're thinking is, "I can't afford a separate phone line," you've got to start thinking differently.

Many successful entrepreneurs will tell you, starting a business comes with some inherent risk. In this case, you're risking a few bucks on a phone line. Wait. Let's take this a step further. I'd like to suggest that paying money for a phone line is an investment . . . not a risk.

If you're still being the ultimate cheapskate, I'd encourage you to do some research. If you go online, you will find many Internet phone companies that provide virtual numbers that come with their own voicemail. I've even seen some for as low as $10 a month. Tell me you haven't spent this much on burritos in one day. Yeah, stop complaining and start making the right moves. Take the time to research how and where you can find an affordable phone service for your business. With such services as Google Voice, you can get your costs down to $0—no excuses, my friend.

Website

This week, a company reached out to me, looking for a jingle. The awesome thing is this is a huge well-known company desiring to create something for a national campaign. I'll get into how to price your jingles later, but for now I can tell you the quote I gave this company reached well into five figures . . . and it didn't even so much as bat an eye on the price.

I'm not telling this story to show off; but to explain that this inquiry came directly from my website. Yep. While I was off doing other things, my website was working 24/7 to promote my company.

Imagine having a website that brings you this type of action from time to time!

Please don't misunderstand; having a website is not magic. People will not mysteriously gravitate to your site just because you have one. It takes work to get it to the point where it will do that. You have to design your site, optimize it, and do a host of other things to make it appealing to visitors.

Sounds like work? It is! As I told you at the very beginning of this book, if you are willing to put in the effort, you will see results. Most people are not! When I start talking about things that might be a bit tougher for you to get your head around, don't wimp out. Decide that you will push forward and do everything necessary for success in this business. Also be mindful that you don't have to do all of these things in one day. Just make up your mind that you will start working toward these goals.

Invest in a website; you can do so many things with it: market your business, show off your work, feature testimonials, collect customer e-mails, and so much more!

References

No matter how many jingles I compose, I always come across clients who ask for references. You would think handing people my extensive jingle demo would be enough, right? Wrong! Understandably, some customers simply want to know how your service has worked for other people. To be more specific, these skeptics, as you may see them, are looking to validate your trustworthiness. Remember: We are dealing with a musical service that has an average price tag of several thousand dollars. So, don't take personal offense at these requests. I would want to check on the safety of my investment, too!

If you're new to the jingle world, you are most likely wondering how you are going to come upon references when you've yet to land your first jingle contract. In instances like this, you have to get a little creative. One solution may be getting written reviews from gigs you've played. No, these are not jingle reviews; however, the praise lavished on your musical skills, be it from a bar owner or a fan, can go quite far in establishing credibility.

Another cool way to scoop up credible reviews is to open up a ReverbNation account. After posting a few of your tunes, I can all but guarantee you'll have people wandering through your profile, offering kind words for your musicianship. Just know many of these people are looking for you to reciprocate praise on their profile page too. It's just a part of the ecosystem on this particular site—scratch my back, I'll scratch yours. But, hey, a small price to pay for a collection of people you can truthfully quote.

When you finally land your first jingle contract, be sure to milk your new business relationship for all its worth. Get a referral from your real live jingle customer!

Be sure to request a written review shortly after finishing up and plaster the positive words from your client everywhere you can: website, e-mail signature, social media, wherever . . .

Brochure

As you begin to market your jingle company, I'm certain you will be asked to furnish some documentation on your services. This means you should have a digital brochure ready to go.

The client you encounter may want to share details about your jingle company with colleagues; this person may want to do some comparisons, or may simply want to have contact details to refer to when looking to speak with you at a later time.

Just the other day I got a call from a company that needed someone to create a jingle for a steak restaurant. The person that contacted me was a middleman, of sorts. This individual's job was to collect information for those who would actually choose the creator of the jingle. Guess what? He wanted some type of literature to pass on to the final decision maker. As I'd been down this road hundreds of times, I had something to give him right away.

Having a brochure at the ready does a few things for you: it speaks to your professionalism, it shows that there is structure within your company, and it also increases your ability to respond quickly when asked.

A brochure does not have to be an elaborate feat of graphic design. It should simply outline the high points of what you offer. As you draft your brochure, *do not* include too much information. Adding a lot of details may be overwhelming for those who simply want to know the basics. On the other hand, you want to be sure not to skimp on what matters. That said, here are a list of things your brochure should include:

- Name of your business
- Contact info: phone, web, and e-mail

- Outline of services; e.g., rock jingles, custom music, sound effects, and so on
- Main selling points; e.g., original compositions, Nashville vocalists, 100 percent acoustic instrumentation, or whatever you can hang your hat on
- Pricing structure: buyouts, one-time fees, licensed music
- Supporting info: how many edits will be given, turnaround times, a brief client list, etc.

Your brochure should be no more than a half-page. Although I have outlined quite a few areas here, know that each of these areas can be expanded upon by including brief bullet points—that's all. There's no reason to write a novel about each of the areas mentioned. Your job is to concisely show who you are to a prospective client.

When you're finished, save your document on your phone, tablet or computer, and have it ready to go when someone asks.

12

NOW WHAT?

At this point, you've been given the groundwork for launching your jingle company. Now the money will just magically fall into your hands, right? Not quite.

Allow me to circle back to one of the primary reasons for writing this book. Musicians have no idea how this business works. That is why I get calls from people looking to write jingles for *my* jingle company. They think the next logical step to success in this business is calling up a would-be competitor and asking for a musical handout. What they don't know, and you'll now learn, is *finding jingle clients is tough*. It takes a lot of time, energy, and smarts to uncover a viable client. When I happen to come across a good-paying customer, do you think for one moment I'm going to share my plunder fifty-fifty with some random music producer who calls me out of nowhere? No, and you wouldn't, either. I worked hard to build the infrastructure, rapport, repertoire, and everything else that allows my business to thrive.

With that bit of common sense underfoot, let's prepare to take the road less traveled—a road that happens to be paved with a lot of cash.

Let's build your jingle business.

13

WHO WILL BUY YOUR JINGLES?

Success with jingles comes down to basic economics—supply and demand.

At this point, you have the basic pieces to *supply* the jingle. Now we need to take a look at those who *demand* this powerful marketing tool.

The following is an overview of the various parties you can approach so as to make the money we've discussed. Although there may be a few more niches to explore, these are the groups most interested in hearing about your jingles:

- Businesses
- Advertising agencies
- Production houses
- Radio/TV/cable broadcasters

You're all dressed up . . . now it's time to go. So, let's get to it!

Businesses

Back in geometry class, I recall my instructor telling us the shortest distance between two points is a straight line. Well, selling a jingle follows the same principle. I invite you to go straight to who wants your jingle: a business! Why get a whole bunch of middlemen involved if you don't have to? Now, if only I can find a place for trigonometry in the real world, I'll have it made.

Wait a minute. You probably didn't need a book to tell you contacting businesses about the purchase of a jingle would be a logical step, right? The real issue here is *how* to approach a business. Which businesses should you target? Who do you ask for when contacting these companies? For many, this proposition is so daunting, giving up before ever starting is the route most traveled.

So, let's get to my first piece of advice when approaching businesses.

GO LOCAL

Target smaller local businesses—*smaller* meaning businesses based in your city or town. Before going any further, I already know that you may want to write jingles for the likes of Burger King and Budweiser. For now, cool your jets on the big dogs. I promise I'll get to how to approach them in a short while. Meanwhile, when you approach smaller establishments, you benefit by circumventing some of the bureaucratic red tape that is inherent to approaching large, nationally branded businesses.

Over the years, I've been approached by a ton of people wanting to sell a jingle to McDonald's, or a company of similar size. A corporation of this magnitude is globally recognized and becomes an obvious target for those looking to make money. As a result, it has rings and rings of personnel, designed to handle the sheer number of inquiries from would-be vendors such as yourself. Don't think for a moment you'll hop on the phone with one of these behemoths and be immediately directed to the right person.

You see, large companies usually hire an advertising agency to deal with all things relating to marketing and creative activities. In fact, some larger enterprises hire *multiple* agencies. Companies of this caliber can be recognized by one or more of the following: they are listed on a stock exchange, they have locations in multiple states, they have a global footprint, and/or they have franchises. Again, the advice when just starting is: *slow your roll.*

Look, I'm not discouraging you from shooting for the stars; I simply want you to build a foundation first. For that reason, I highly recommend starting with lower-hanging fruit—smaller businesses. Examples of these businesses are: car dealerships, dentists, lawyers, diners, funeral homes, and so on.

So, let's talk about how to uncover some clients for your jingle company.

TAKE A LOOK AROUND

One of the fastest ways to find businesses that need jingles is to do a bit of research by watching and listening—to TV and radio, to be more specific.

When I first started my jingle company, it was common practice for me to keep a notepad nearby while watching or listening to shows and other programming. As locally produced commercials came on, I'd make notes on the company—name of business, its phone number, website, what it offered, and so on.

As I listened to these companies, I'd keep my ear attuned to notice ads that did not have a jingle. That's all it took for me to begin building a list of reasonable places to call. It's just that simple.

Let me reiterate and be specific: start off with companies you hear on radio or TV. Just be sure to scan through all stations in your area, as to uncover as many opportunities as you can. Avoid businesses that you haven't heard over the airwaves—such companies likely advertise with direct mail, Google ads, e-mail campaigns, billboards, and so on. Presenting jingles to businesses that are *not* on the air may be a tough sale. It's sort of like buying Broadway tickets for your first date before getting the courage to ask that beautiful girl out. In other words, a business that is not using broadcast or streaming media is a far tougher target to hit, as the means for airing the jingle has yet to be established.

With that in mind, understand that businesses that are on air are your primary target; they already have skin in the game. Your job, at this point, is to nudge them in your direction by showing them a better way of advertising—with a memorable jingle, no less.

I once recall hearing an ad from a local county agency. This agency was attempting to encourage listeners to participate in a carpooling/ride-sharing program. I heard commercials from this organization a number of times. However, one day, the lightbulb finally went on in my mind and I thought, *Why don't I call these guys and see if they'd be open to using a jingle to make their message stand out and stick?*

Sure enough, I gathered the agency's contact info and picked up the phone. After placing a few calls and gently prodding the receptionist with questions, I located Lynn, the person in charge of making the radio commercials I had been hearing all that time. After a brief conversation, guess what happened? To my surprise, Lynn and the agency promptly invited me downtown for a further discussion! Without even having made a dime, I was completely ecstatic. My simple plan of copying down viable local companies was off to a great start. A few more meetings and brainstorming sessions later, this agency ended up hiring me to make the carpooling jingle. I wound up securing a $3,200 paycheck—a pretty sweet reward for *listening* to the radio!

I already said that the absence of bureaucracy and red tape are prime advantages of starting *small* or going local. But also, there's the benefit of proximity. In the previous example, I talked about calling the business, but the next step was a visit to the business. When you deal with local businesses, you will have the ability to see the client in person; this works in your favor. Face-to-face conversations offer a substantial boost to selling jingles. It's something I've experienced time and time again. Although you can leverage online technology and be successful selling jingles to businesses all over the globe (a topic I will get to in "The Bonus Round" chapter), I feel it necessary to walk you through what I've seen work firsthand.

WHERE TO LOOK

Let's dig into the types of business you can target in your area.

Although the following is not an exhaustive list, it should be enough to give you ideas as to which local businesses have been known to use jingles:

- Car/motorcycle/motorsports/RV dealers
- Local banks/credit unions/mortgage companies
- Dentists/chiropractors/eye doctors/hospitals/clinics
- Cosmetic surgeons/hair salons/spas
- Gyms/weight-loss groups
- Restaurants/bakeries/diners/bars/clubs
- Festivals/fairs/zoos/activity centers
- Furniture stores/antiques dealers/pawnshops

All the aforementioned groups could potentially represent hundreds, if not thousands, of businesses within a 50-mile radius of where you live—that's a lot! Again, we haven't even begun talking about doing business outside of your town yet. And remember, I said my list was not exhaustive.

LASER FOCUS

The number of local opportunities is awesome because you can begin to see that there are a lot of places to make cash.

The downside is that it's tough to bc successful when the sheer number of places to do business can pose as a massive distraction.

Given this reality, I'd like to offer this simple, yet effective advice:

> Target one group or industry at a time. Become a specialist in that area.

As you decide to focus on one group, go back to my earlier advice: create a demonstration of your work—a made-up jingle aimed at that group.

Let me give you an example to put things into focus.

Say we choose dentists as our primary target. You would, of course, produce a faux-jingle demo geared toward those in this profession.

When you go with this approach, as opposed to using a jingle designed for another industry, you're able to quickly help the would-be client imagine what it would be like to have a jingle for his or her specific dental practice. This leaves less to the imagination and fewer obstacles for you to overcome.

What I just outlined for you has been a tough lesson that I had to learn over time. I've always thought that people would just recognize hot music when they heard it, no matter what type of business it relates to. I can tell you firsthand, this notion is wrong. Keep in mind, you will have many clients who don't consider themselves to be all that "creative." As a result, you will essentially have to spell things out for them—create music that is very close to what their business can use. Be patient and remember that you are the musician in the relationship, not them. A large part of your earning potential will be based on bridging this communication gap.

So, buy in to the idea of targeting one industry at a time and create a jingle demo for the group you choose.

Now, I want to briefly touch on another pertinent point.

BE RELEVANT

For your jingle demo to stand out within specific industries, your lyrical content must resonate with the group you choose, not only in subject matter but also in rhetoric. Every industry has certain buzzwords, selling points, and jargon. If you're able to expertly craft a jingle with such content, you will capture attention and interest. By doing so, you're demonstrating that you can skillfully fuse concepts from your clients' trade with memorable music from yours.

For example, many car dealerships I've worked with have wanted to hear such things as *service*, *selection*, *unbeatable deals*, *standing by promises*, *reputation*, *integrity*, and so on. So when creating a jingle demo, I would, of course, figure out a way to get some of that verbiage paired with the music.

It's incumbent upon you to do a bit of research to determine the type of lyrics you should include. Research could be as simple as searching on YouTube, or turning on the TV or radio and listening to existing jingles for the area you've selected.

If you're going to target cosmetic surgeons, as an example, proactively seek out jingles in this industry and find out what others are doing.

Look up and search around websites for the industry you've chosen. Oftentimes, homepages will reveal a treasure trove of the terms you'll need.

If you are looking to put your efforts into overdrive, I highly recommend you go even deeper than surface-level terminology.

I recently had a meeting with an insurance company that was looking to have a jingle developed. As we started the meeting, I was asked for the typical stuff: samples of my work, a synopsis of my experience, and pricing. However, as the meeting went on, I began to ask the owner questions about *his* business. These weren't nebulous, off-the-wall questions, but industry-specific questions. I asked if the firm specialized in home, auto, or life insurance, if it were a broker for one insurer or could shop multiple carriers, and my questions went on from there. By asking such questions, the owner quickly knew he was dealing with a person who had an understanding of his world. He felt like I "got it." Instead of me begging for a shot at making a jingle for his business, the meeting ended with him asking, "What should I do? What do you recommend for the jingle?" His questions made it clear that *I was the expert* in his eyes.

Here's the kicker: I was initially told my prices were a bit higher than some others he'd reached out to, but the strong display of my competence made the angst over the bigger price tag vanish. All of this was achieved by acquiring a rudimentary understanding of his industry.

For instance, did you know that a dentist could ask you to sing about *implants* in a jingle? Did you know that dentists were even allowed to give people implants? They're called *dental implants*. What were you thinking, huh? C'mon, tell the truth. Were you thinking of a different type of implant? It's all right—don't beat yourself up. Just know that I'm looking to prove that the lack of basic info about a business could result in you appearing ill-informed. This kind of embarrassment is totally cool among friends; however, such a misstep while trying to establish credibility for your jingle company may not turn out so well.

It will serve you well to learn about the sector you wish to target. Read a few articles, watch some videos, or pick up a book or two to give yourself a working knowledge of the group you're focusing on. If that sounds way too daunting, choose a sector you already have some knowledge of. Have you ever worked at a doctor's office, restaurant, college, moving company, or some other business? Go after the industry you've had exposure to. What do you remember about what these businesses did and what was important to them? Understand that I'm *not* sending you off to become an absolute expert in these industries. However, I do suggest you be able to have a conversation with a business client and not embarrass yourself due to ignorance.

THE RIGHT PEOPLE

When contacting smaller businesses, you will be looking for the following key people:

- The owner
- The head marketing person
- The coach/advocate

Let's talk about the role and importance of each.

THE OWNER

In smaller companies, it is likely the owner of the company is deeply involved with all aspects of the business—especially marketing. Jingles, of course, will fit into that category. Also, it is likely the owner will be the one footing the bill for your services, so this is the person you want to be in contact with right from the start, if at all possible.

Now that you know this, what should you do? Pick up the phone and ask for the owner!

"Whoa," you say? Okay, I know this may be a little intimidating, but we're looking for the shortest distance between two points, remember? To set your mind at ease, I'll discuss *what* to say in just a moment. Before I do, let's cover who else could appear on our call list, especially if the owner is not available.

HEAD OF MARKETING

Contact the marketing department; more specifically, the head of the marketing department.

Job titles can be quite confusing. Those who work in marketing can carry any number of titles: chief marketing officer (CMO), VP of branding, creative director, and the list goes on. Let's not get thrown off by such descriptors. All we really care about is *who is in charge of marketing*—that's it. So, when you call a small business, your question will be just as simple. You're going to ask the following question: "Will you put me in contact with the person who heads up advertising for your company, please?"

I know, I know. You don't know what to say yet. We're almost to the point of discussing what to do when these people answer the phone. But first, let's talk about one more person you ought to know—the coach or advocate.

THE COACH/ADVOCATE

A coach or advocate is some nice soul who works for a company and feeds you inside information—info which will assist you in finding the person within the company who would authorize the purchase of a jingle. These advocates can hand you treasured insight that will put you on the fast track to selling your services.

The main difficulty in locating coaches and advocates is they are not walking around with neon signs over their head. To find these people, you have to be perceptive. Watch out for the person in the company who is superchatty. Look for those who are friendly and easy to speak with—no matter what their position at the business. That person can be a janitor or the floor manager, the IT guy or a regional coordinator. Their function at the company is not the main thing; it's their willingness to share inside knowledge about connecting with their company.

A short while ago I spoke with a guy at an auto collision shop here in town. This gentleman was completely into the idea of getting a jingle for their business. As the conversation went on, there was one glaring problem: this guy had absolutely no authority to purchase a jingle on his company's behalf. At first I was kind of annoyed that I had spent so much time with him, trying to explain my service, but I soon realized this man was my coach/advocate. He began to tell me about the owner, the company's marketing needs, and internal discussions about jingles. In fact, he ended up giving me the owner's mobile number and the best time to call.

The beauty of this setup is that when I called the owner, I was able to say something like, "Hi, George! One of your employees by the name of Tom recommended I reach out to you about designing a jingle for your radio ads. Do you have a moment?"

I immediately went from being a complete stranger to someone his employee regarded as useful to his company, a far cry from being an unknown caller.

Advertising Agencies

There's no question; calling businesses is a solid way of finding clients. However, it is my experience that contacting individual businesses can take quite a bit of time and effort. When you call a business, you have to maneuver your way through to the right people in the company (as described in the previous section). Once you've found the right contacts, you are now hoping to immediately set up a meeting and ultimately close the deal. The reality is that you will have to make multiple calls, deal with people being busy, and be asked to call back on a regular basis. This is the part of the business that totally debilitates noobs, novices, and newcomers. Understand that this process will occupy a fair amount of your time. When it's all said and done, you may have only reached *one* business. This is not a bad thing if that business wants your jingle. If they do not, you have to start at square one with another company, and then another, and so on. It is quite easy to feel as though you're searching for a needle in a Jupiter-size haystack.

Don't let this reality deflate your enthusiasm and optimism regarding your success in selling jingles. Remember, I've seen the bigger picture and want to offer you some shortcuts.

With that in mind, let's talk about a potentially better way of finding people who want your jingles.

Instead of hunting around looking for businesses who want jingles, what if you were able to have someone do the hunting for you? You can. It's time for you to develop a relationship with an *advertising agency*.

In case you didn't know, ad agencies are companies that market and promote businesses. Their very existence is based on whether they have clients to advertise for.

Understand that ad agencies can vary in size. Some agencies are global, multibillion-dollar operations, whereas others are just one or two guys working out of their garage. In either case, it is imperative that you start to build a relationship with an advertising agency. That's because most agencies do not create music in-house. In other words, you're *not* likely to find a staff composer or salaried musician working at an agency. In the vast majority of instances, ad agencies *hire* music companies on behalf of clients they are providing services for.

While I'm on the subject, let me throw in something totally confusing: most large ad agencies that use music for advertising campaigns have someone in-house called a *music producer*. I just finished telling you that most large agencies outsource music. What's up with the music producer situation? In the ad agency world, think of music producers as music curators or licensors. In many instances, they are responsible for assembling music resources for commercials. From what I've seen, these people are *nothing* like music producers you've heard about that work in studios with artists. Keep that in mind as you begin to interact with larger advertising agencies.

Due to the fact that the music producers at these marketing firms don't actually create music, there is an inherent need for people like you and me. It's a codependent ecosystem that benefits both parties.

With that being said, let's talk about one of the biggest benefits of partnering with an ad agency. Depending on their size, these firms can have anywhere from dozens to hundreds of businesses they are working for at any given time. These businesses are having commercials made, many of which require music. The music in these commercials is being created by people outside the agency. I think you know what I'm hinting at, right?

Becoming a trusted music/jingle creator for an advertising agency could be a never-ending stream of substantial income for you!

Essentially, *one relationship opens the door to many.*

Years ago, I established a business relationship with a media company on the East Coast. Every time this firm needs a jingle, it calls me. It's just that simple. I don't have to hunt it down. I don't have to go through some elaborate presentation when we speak. When I see its number on my caller ID, I get pretty excited because I know it has already decided to hire me. It's just a matter of writing down a few details and providing its client with a deadline for a jingle's first draft. The awesome part of such relationships is that I can spend my time on other projects while agencies, such as the one I partner with, are promoting me to their clients.

> Seek a single point of contact that offers access to multiple opportunities.

Are you excited? You should be. But before you start beating down the door of every ad agency, let's cover a few things that will help you along the way.

First, know that you should not approach *every* advertising firm out there.

There are many types of ad agencies. There are ones that specialize in print, social media, packaging, and media buying. There are firms that deal with major corporations; others work with mom-and-pop establishments. You'll also learn there are agencies that specialize in certain demographics—Latino population, women, kids, seniors, and so on.

So let's talk about the ad agencies you need to approach.

Only contact ad agencies that specialize in *broadcast advertising*—radio, TV, and cable. You can also include those that create online and corporate videos. By choosing the types of agencies, you can all but guarantee that music will be an essential building block for the commercials they make.

When I first started my jingle company, I thought *every* marketing firm made TV ads and radio commercials. That's simply not the case. I once called an ad agency and started to ramble on about how great my jingles were. The people I spoke with sounded totally confused; they couldn't understand why I was calling. I, on the other hand, was like, "So, you never heard of jingles before? Aren't you an ad agency?!" I came to find out the agency I called specialized in magazine ads. All of their marketing was centered on Photoshopping and airbrushing models, and creating graphic designs—visual advertising techniques. How would my jingles have benefited their clients? My services were *not* a fit for this particular type of agency. As annoying as this was at the time, I soon embraced the truth that I was barking up the wrong tree.

When it comes to developing a relationship with ad agencies that work in the areas of TV, radio, cable, and online marketing, you have three general ad agency categories: large, midsize, and small/boutique.

There are a number of ways to find these agencies. Here are a few recommendations:

- Google "full service advertising agency" or search your city's name + "ad agency."
- Search for agencies at the American Association of Advertising Agencies website, www.AAAA.org.
- Call businesses you've seen or heard on the radio, TV, or cable and ask for the name of the ad agency representing them.
- Read up on prominent agencies at Ad Age's website, www.adage.com.

As you begin discovering agencies to reach out to, you'll notice there are a ton of them out there. It may feel overwhelming (similar to what I described when calling businesses directly). Given that reality, I will offer familiar advice: focus on one part of the picture—not the entire thing. Start your journey by focusing on smaller agencies around town or the state. Sure, you can go big and go after the trendy West Coast firms, but that's a huge hill to climb when first starting off. No matter what you decide, just choose a direction and stick with it. I offer this advice to help you get focused. If you bounce around and make calls to major agencies and then small ones, you're going to find vastly different audiences, requiring vastly different strategies.

THE BIG FISH

Let's talk about going after large agencies.

Earlier, I alluded to the fact that agencies that represent big global brands are *big fish*. Understand that hauling in such a catch may take some time, effort and potentially a lot of schmoozing. But in the end it will feel great cashing a check that could literally equal several months, if not a year of pay from your typical gig.

Jingle composers would love to make music for huge corporations—such as McDonald's, Toyota, IBM, and the list goes on. Such aspirations are well founded, as landing a jingle contract with large companies would most likely net you a five-figure paycheck—maybe more. Understand that operating at such a level is not a mere walk in the park. Your work has to be incredibly good! You're probably thinking, "Oh, it's good!" Before you drop the mic and begin strutting around the room like a boss, know that you are competing with high-caliber musicians and studios from around the globe—talent from Los Angeles, New York, Nashville, London . . . you name it. Your would-be competitors may come to the table with an extensive network of A-list clients from all over the world. Some of these music creators have also worked with internationally known singers and bands. So, don't think for a moment these rivals are meaningless. I am not mentioning this reality to instill fear or hopelessness; I'm simply drawing your attention to the truth of the situation. You have to be exceptional at your craft: the sound, quality, structure, melody, content, and so on.

A few years ago, I was having my music reviewed by an advertising company out in Los Angeles. As I spoke with the guy at this company, I felt that my music would easily make the cut. At this time, my jingle company was pretty established, and I had quite a few success stories and solid work to show off. To my surprise, I was rejected. This slap-down prompted me to ask why I didn't make the cut. The guy I spoke with said, "Listen, there are a lot of big producers out here in L.A. When they are between albums, they send me stuff"—meaning their high-end music tracks. I was surprised. Why would Grammy-nominated producers be making music for ads? Don't they have bigger projects to work on? These questions boiled in my mind. But you know what? The answer didn't really matter. It just meant that I had to step things up if these big names were and will continue to be a part of the landscape, producing music for advertising.

That, as I said, was a few years ago. But now it all makes sense. With the emergence of streaming and illegal file sharing, physical and digital album sales are way down. Do you think these monster-size producers are making the same type of money they were raking in during the '80s and '90s, given today's technology? No. They have thoughtfully begun to migrate to where the dollars are.

So, just know working with massive ad agencies requires that you come with your A-game.

Next, let's talk about another subject you're most likely to run into when approaching huge agencies: *protection.* You see, when large corporations advertise, they open themselves up to a lot of things: competitor reprisal, consumer criticism, knockoffs/copycats, and the most egregious of them all, *lawsuits.* In this day and age, there is always a guy who is willing to trip on his own shoelaces or fling himself into the shelves at a Walmart store, in hopes of filing a frivolous lawsuit. People are sue-happy—looking for an easy paycheck. Major corporations know this. As a result, they do everything possible to insulate themselves from such financial liability.

This protective mind-set trickles down to even their advertising. Agencies that work on behalf of renowned brands have to be insured and are forced to use vendors that are insured, too. In this case, you would be the music vendor. Do you find this fact confusing? Are you thinking, "What does being sued have to do with me and insurance?" Stick with me for a moment. Let's answer these questions with an example.

Imagine that you succeeded in becoming a jingle producer for Burger King's ad agency. Let's also say they came to you and wanted something incredibly catchy to outshine its largest competitor (whoever *that* may be). In response to this request, you develop what you feel is the most brilliant jingle of a generation. It goes like this, "Ba, da, da, da, daah . . . I'm *grubbin'* it!" For some odd reason, the agency and Burger King has crowned you a creative genius. That is, until they are summarily sued by McDonald's for copyright infringement. You're informed that your jingle is quite similar to "I'm Lovin' It." As the legal pooh coalesces and rolls downhill, who do you think will be in the direct path of this warm, brown snowball? Yeah, that would be *you*—balled up in a corner like an abused stray.

I'm sure you are aware that lawsuits at the corporate level are not exactly cheap, so when it comes to dealing with multinational powerhouses, most agencies insist on a bit of protection for their backsides. In this example, Burger King would blame the agency for the infringement issue; in turn the agency would point the finger at you.

This elaborate example leads to something you're going to need if you want to rock with the big boys: *E&O insurance.*

E&O is short for *errors and omissions*. According to Investopedia.com,

> E&O insurance is: a professional liability insurance that protects companies and individuals against claims made by clients for inadequate work or negligent actions. Errors and omissions insurance often covers both court costs and any settlements up to the amount specified on the insurance contract.[1]

It is my experience that many of the large agencies won't give you two seconds unless you have this insurance. Possessing this coverage inherently demonstrates that you are ready to hang with leading innovators. If you want operate at this level, know that most likely you will be asked to produce proof of this insurance.

As I've said with other hurdles posed in this book, don't let this idea deflate your enthusiasm. By reason of spending time with this guide, you have indicated that you want to learn how to make it in this business. Well, guess what? This is a part of what it takes to operate at a high level. Sometimes, you have to make a small investment in yourself, if you're truly serious.

But let's deal with reality. Money can be a bit scarce at times, *even* when you're serious, right? The point of this book is *how* to find this elusive cash. So, if the idea of paying for an insurance policy seems a bit daunting, let me share a hidden nugget that may help you, in the form of a personal experience.

As I was getting my jingle company off the ground a few years back, I decided that I wanted to reach for the stars. I found an ad agency that represented a lot of nationally and internationally known brands—the big names in retail, fast food, home improvement, and so on. To make a long story short, I eventually landed a phone conference with the music decision maker at this Chicago-based agency. The interested woman at this ad agency began to ask me for more details about my jingle company. I enthusiastically seized on every question and happily provided, what I felt, were the right answers. My confidence rose quickly as we spoke. I felt that I was on my way to recording the next memorable jingle for a major company. But the world stopped with these next few words: "Do you have E&O insurance?" Honestly, the question came so fast, I didn't understand what was being said. "Do I have *what*?" I asked, seeking clarification. There it was; the very first time I ever heard the term. The fun times stalled rather abruptly. Of course, I was turned away shortly after revealing I was clueless on the topic. I was left stunned; I couldn't understand why we weren't talking about music any more. This lady seemed fixated on, what I thought was, a trivial technicality.

Months after this incident, I developed a friendly relationship with a staff member at a different agency. This person began to school me on the ins and outs of working with larger agencies; he became my *coach.* When the subject of this insurance came up, he mentioned that there was a way to deal with this impasse. I came to learn that some agencies will allow a one-time exception for the absence of this insurance. If they do, many will insist on the coverage moving forward. If you cannot find any takers for this provision, some will allow you to begin work with an agreement to acquire the insurance before the project airs.

With the previous story in mind, I recommend the following tip:

Ask to make a contingency arrangement with the agency you're seeking to do business with. Commit to obtaining E&O insurance at the time the firm agrees to hire you for a real project.

TALKING MONEY

I already mentioned that big agencies most likely deal with major studios and musicians all the time, so after determining that you can deliver on the right sound, agencies don't want to talk about your outboard gear, pickups on your guitar, or the type of condenser mic you have—they'll want to talk dollars and cents. The reason for the quick jump to a money discussion is that agencies run each commercial project off a *budget.* Most commercials have been assigned a predetermined amount of money for various parts of their construction. For instance, a TV commercial project will have a set amount of money allocated for such things as a producer, actors, animator, camera people, director, copywriter, and so on. Within these budgets, you're likely to find an amount of money that has been specifically earmarked for music. Sometimes, this amount is small; other times, this amount can be staggering. As a result, ad agencies will most likely talk money to figure out whether you'll fit into their plans. Please note: *Don't assume any talk of money means you've got the deal.* It's simply a screening mechanism to save the agency from wasting time with music providers they can't afford.

Now let's talk about the people you want to speak with at an agency. Earlier I mentioned the *music producer*. This is definitely one person you want to reach at an agency, but there are several other titles I want to introduce you to. You may not find a music producer at every single ad agency, though the agency creates broadcast or online commercials. In their absence, here are a few people you can ask for:

- Music supervisor
- Creative director
- TV or radio producer
- Video producer/editor
- "Someone in the broadcast department"
- "Someone in the postproduction department"
- "The person that licenses music for the agency"

Considering the structure of any given agency, you may come across a few more variants. However, these, along with music producers, are the main ones to ask for so you can start a conversation about jingles with the right person.

Production Houses

Production houses are media-based businesses that create marketing content for a variety of groups: businesses, ad agencies, government entities, and so on. Sometimes people confuse production houses with ad agencies because they both appear to be places where ads are developed. Although video- and audio-based commercials can be produced from within an ad agency, a lot of this type of work is farmed out. Agencies will typically hire production houses to take on a particular campaign or assignment. This explains how an ad agency based in New York can furnish an ad that's filmed in, say, Miami. The agency simply hires a production company in South Beach that specializes in what they're looking for.

Having said all that, production houses are places to approach about your jingles. They are the ones who put together the actual media content for any given ad—video, graphics, and . . . *music*!

Whenever I talk about production houses, my mind cues the dream-sequence music as I reminisce about my very first break in the jingle business. As you might have guessed, I got my first jingle assignment from a local production house. In fact, this company wound up having me work on three or four projects in my first year of business. For a guy who was unemployed at the time, several thousand dollars in jingle checks felt pretty nice.

Right there in your area may be companies like the one I found when I first got started. Open a search engine and type in the name of your city followed by the words "production companies." If your town is large enough, chances are you will begin to see a whole host of prospects for your business that you hadn't known about until now.

The great part about all of this is that you're not limited to production houses in your own city. As an example, there's a sizable production house in Philadelphia that I've worked with for years. After ten-plus years of doing business with the owner of the production house, I would not recognize him if I bumped into him on the street; we've never met face-to-face! But you know what? Our relationship is pretty strong. This partnership has netted my company tens of thousands of dollars over the years. So, let that be a lesson to you: your location is not a barrier. We'll dig into that topic a bit later.

Radio/TV/Cable Broadcasters

You're likely to hear jingles while on hold when calling a company. You can hear them on company websites and YouTube. However, the place that you're most likely to hear them is over the airwaves—radio, TV, and cable.

Given where we are now with social media and other digital technology, you may have been led to believe that broadcast media is dying—an old dinosaur gasping for its final breath. I'd argue that it is not dead and is, in fact, your primary target for your jingle business.

Allow me to qualify my stance on this.

If you were to hop into your car right now and take a short drive, you'd be able to tune into a handful of local radio stations while cruising, right? If, for instance, you wanted to know about the latest horrific crime in your town, your local TV station is happy to oblige . . . *news at eleven*! If we were to count up all these stations in your town and account for both radio and TV stations in every city in the United States, we'd be looking at *thirty thousand-plus* media outlets. Each and every one of these stations represents anywhere from a few dozen to one hundred–plus advertisers or sponsors.

In all my years in the business, I've rarely heard of any of these stations' going belly up—closing up shop and departing forever. Sure, I've seen smooth jazz music stations become top-forty hits stations. I've also witnessed stations be acquired by other media companies. But stations disappearing in droves? No.

I recognize that revenue for these media outlets has suffered as online and mobile marketing have taken hold, but to say that broadcast advertising is dead, despite it being a multibillion-dollar industry, means you've chosen to ignore the evidence that can be found in your own backyard.

So, let's dive into why your local broadcasters may be a gold mine for your business.

As stated earlier, I'd rather you establish one relationship that gives way to many others. This concept falls squarely into the *work-smarter* philosophy.

If you are able to forge a relationship with a local station, it may give you access to its roster of businesses that are or will be advertising on its airwaves.

But why would a station potentially give you access to its clients? The answer is simple: Businesses need advertising that stands out. If an ad stands out on a station, the audience remembers and acts upon it. This business is more likely to purchase more advertising space from the station. If a station recognizes that you are capable of writing jingles that can grab listeners' attention, you become someone who can help it reach its ultimate goal of selling more advertising. It's a symbiotic relationship.

CONTACTING THE RIGHT PEOPLE

Now that I've convinced you that your local stations are great places to get businesses interested in your jingles, who's the right person to speak with? *Start with the sales department.*

Now, the idea of contacting a person in the sales department at a station may seem counter-intuitive or unrelated, at best. I can assure you it's not. Remember, a local station is looking to *sell* advertising space—it's called *airtime*. This provides the funding that keeps broadcasters operational. If your jingle can help make businesses' commercials better, you will become the station's best friend—*the friend of the broadcast sales department*!

There are three major sales roles at most stations that you need to know about. Please note the following roles will be the same for radio, TV, and cable broadcasters. I took the liberty of including the acronyms for these roles, as they are used quite often among those in the industry.

GENERAL SALES MANAGER (GSM) OR DIRECTOR OF SALES (DOS)

The GSM or DOS usually serves as the head of the sales department at any given station. When reaching out to a station, try making this person your first point of contact. The head of a sales department is always on the lookout for resources or services that will aid his or her staff in serving clients better and will, most important, generate revenue for the station. If you can demonstrate that your jingle production is worthwhile, the GSM or DOS has the authority to mandate that the entire sales department partner with your company, making you the exclusive jingle maker for businesses that want them.

I once forged such a relationship with a GSM by the name of Tom at an Orlando TV station. He liked my music so much that his sales team of about eighteen people was told to offer my jingles to all of the businesses it worked with. I ended up making many thousands of dollars through this station, simply because the GSM believed in what I had to offer.

LOCAL SALES MANAGER (LSM)

If you move one level down in the hierarchy, you're likely to find two roles: local sales manager and national sales manager.

For our purposes, *do not* engage with the national sales manager, as the scope of this person's sales duties will render your jingles meaningless. You see, national sales managers are responsible for selling airtime to national businesses that wish to advertise in any given city. For instance, if Pepsi wanted to air ads in Memphis, it, or a media company/buyer that represents the soft drink giant, would contact a national sales manager at a Memphis station and place the order for commercials. The reason you do not contact national sales managers about making jingles is because their large clients, such as Taco Bell, Lowe's, and so on, have already had the content of their ads (including music) crafted by their advertising agencies.

To get in on this type of *national* action, you'd have to back down a few steps and target ad agencies representing these large brands long before their ads arrive at a local station. (See "The Big Fish" section, page 86.)

Now that you know talking with the national sales manager is a dead-end road, make an effort to reach out to the local sales manager. The LSM is responsible for generating relationships and managing sales people who focus on all of the small to midsize businesses in their respective city. The LSM typically reports to the GSM, DOS, or in some cases, the general manager. Although the LSM may not have absolute authority over the sales department, such individuals can be quite influential in giving you a chance to work with the station's advertisers. If the head of the sales department can't be reached, an LSM is always a great option. In fact, I make it a practice of reaching out to both the GSM and LSM at the same time.

ACCOUNT EXECUTIVE (AE)

An AE is a salesperson at a station. Usually, AEs don't manage others, but manage their own sales responsibilities. Their job is to go out into the community and find businesses that are willing to advertise with their station. AEs, for the most part, are commissioned salespeople. In other words, if they don't sell airtime, they don't make money. As a result, account executives are always looking to do what they can to persuade businesses to advertise with their station—including offering tools that may benefit perspective customers. In this case, we hope AEs will see your jingle production skills as the very thing they need so as to gain the attention of clients.

Frank, an AE from Tampa, once called and asked whether I'd help with a client he was in talks with—a car dealership. This particular client wanted to freshen up its advertising and needed to further strengthen its branding. Frank immediately recognized that helping this business reach its goals would most certainly aid him in selling more airtime, and by default, help him make more money in commissions. That's when he decided to reach out and have me speak with his client about proposing a jingle package. He wisely deduced that a custom jingle was the marketing nudge this client needed. He was right; I got the jingle contract, and Frank got to sell the dealership more airtime. All three parties were happy.

Creating a mutually beneficial relationship with an AE is probably one of the smartest things you can do to make money as a jingle maker. Both of you are equally hungry to see some action. Your job, at least in the beginning, is to convince this person that your jingles can be a way for you *both* to get want you want.

Now that we've identified viable targets, we need to move to the next sensible step . . . selling yourself and your business!

14

HELLO, MAY I SPEAK TO MONEY?

What is the most powerful way to get your jingle business off the ground? I believe it all starts with a simple phone call.

Yes, there are other ways to find clients, of which we'll get into, but understand that a simple phone call is likely to be your most direct way of seeing cash for your jingle business.

Before going any further, you already may be thinking, "I'd prefer to send an e-mail instead." If that is how you feel, please follow this simple advice: *Stop avoiding direct contact!*

If you are intimidated or uncomfortable making a phone call, *POW!*—you have officially shot yourself in the foot. In others words, *if you're already moving in the direction of dodging people, your business has already failed.*

I once brought in an intern to make sales calls on behalf of our music production company. I provided very clear instructions as to how I wanted him to reach potential customers. You wanna know what we told him to do? You guessed it: pick up the phone and have a conversation! As I sat and watched the intern for several days, I started to see a weird pattern. He would feverishly type away on his laptop in the front office for most of the day. He would be there anywhere from four to six hours, pecking at his computer, squinting his eyeballs out. And just as the day came to a close, he'd get all jittery and make about two phone calls. Then, he'd leave and repeat this same thing the following day. Eventually, I had to ask, "What are you working on?" He told me how he's been sending e-mails, researching companies—scrolling through their websites, and on and on. My reply was to the point, "Hmm. It looks like you don't like making phone calls, right?" Of course, I was right! Although I fully appreciated the tech savvy of this young intern, I felt his inability to emerge from behind an e-mail, tweet, or post was detrimental. This guy's phone phobia kept him from doing what mattered most—picking up the phone and having a good old-fashioned conversation.

Electronic means of communication has its place. However, people have become lazy and avoidant. These people tend to use online correspondence as a crutch rather than a supplemental tool.

An e-mail can remain unopened, be sent to a spam folder, or be ignored. A phone conversation, however, is something that requires engagement—no matter how brief. Why not give yourself the chance to engage with a potential client rather than lobbing e-mails from afar? You know what else? Many other, would-be jingle makers hide behind online communications, too. What if you were different? What if you possessed the courage to get out there and do what others won't?

At the beginning of this book I told you that life's secrets for success are often hiding in plain view. A phone conversation is one of those secrets—so simple, yet so avoided. I can all but guarantee you will see far more income in your jingle business if you can summon the courage to pick up the phone.

Promoting your business via phone is a cheap, yet powerful marketing tool.

One last anecdote about calling prospects.

A company contacted me in search of a quote. At the time I had no idea this company had also reached out to several other jingle providers—looking to have us compete head-to-head without my knowing it. Upon my calling the business, the person at this company said, "You were the only one to actually call us back." Apparently, my music competitors had replied with e-mails only. Although the price of my jingle was a bit more than the other quotes that this company got, the firm felt better about us because there was a real person on the other end—me! Its trust level shot up because my presence on the phone gave the client the assurance that there was a guy out there who was ready to personally walk them through all the steps for getting the perfect sound for its commercial! Hearing a voice on the other end made the person I spoke with feel more comfortable.

Look, if you're not going to have the guts to speak up for your business, it doesn't really matter whether you're the hottest producer, singer, or beat maker. No one will ever know without you being able to communicate. Force yourself to go beyond your comfort zone and talk to people! A conversation may just be the thing that earns you your first paid recording.

If you're still hesitant about making phone calls for fear of coming across as some sleazy telemarketer, don't be. In the US telemarketing restrictions (Do Not Call lists) are put in place primarily to protect *residents* from being harassed in their homes. These prohibitions *do not* apply to one's business (yours) calling another. Have you ever heard the term *business-to-business (B2B) sales*? Well that's what you're doing, providing services for other businesses. So, relax! It's totally legal, and not at all dodgy.

Now I bet I've got you all amped up to make a call—any call, right? You're like, "Bring it!"

Great! Let's focus all of that energy in the right place.

Starting the Conversation

Now that I've convinced you to pick up the phone, let's talk about what to say.

The very best piece of advice I can give you about making your initial call is to *write a script.*

Yup, a script—predetermined written words that will guide you through the initial moments of your conversation.

If you think this sounds too cheesy or undesirable, get over it! Embrace the tough love I'm sending your way and let me remind you that making it in this business requires you do things that may feel a bit uncomfortable.

Quick review: Would you rather feel uneasy and rake in a few thousand dollars or feel the warm, familiar insides of your *empty* pockets?

Okay, enough of the browbeating. Let's get back to building a script.

Please get one thing straight: When you call up a business and offer your jingle services, know that you are *selling*. Yes, you are, in fact, a salesperson. Don't let that moniker make you feel weird or uneasy; it's just the reality of promoting your business. You have to communicate effectively.

As a salesperson, you will need to have a *sales pitch*. You must be able to quickly articulate who you are, what you offer, and why someone should care. All of these things have to be accomplished in a short amount of time, as many of the people you are calling are incredibly busy.

Hopefully, the icky feeling of reading a script will start to diminish as you come to understand the importance of deliberate and concise communication. When you've only got a few seconds to make an impression, it matters that you get to the point while making sense. See this as your elevator pitch.

I remember when I got my first sales job (in a different industry). The main requirement for this position was to use a script when talking to people on the phone. I have to admit, I absolutely hated it. It felt robotic, cheesy, and utterly stupid. I truly felt like the dirtiest of telemarketers. To make things worse, my boss would hang out around my desk, just listening to me stutter all morning. My twisted tongue most likely came from the verbal beat-down I got if I strayed from the script.

As it turned out, having a script was one of the best tools I have ever adopted. I say this in retrospect, of course.

As I read the script on a regular basis, my speech became more natural. Having predetermined lines kept me from getting lost in verbal tics, such as saying "uh" a billion times. The script ensured that I stayed on topic. And you know what? These things resulted in my using the phone with more confidence. The people on the other end immediately knew they were dealing with a guy from a *real* business; not a guy calling from his basement . . . in his underwear.

Hopefully I've convinced you.

In just a moment, I am going to provide a sample script for you to use when selling jingles. Before doing that, I want to outline the building blocks needed for your script.

Your script should include:

- An introduction
- The reason for the call
- Sales pitch

With the previous points in mind, write your script out. I repeat, *write it out*! Please don't fight me on this—just do it. The goal is for you to keep seeing the words and to practice until you come across as natural and conversational. As you write things out, don't get too fancy or colorful with your words; you're not calling to demo your thesaurus.

A final word on this: Your script should be pretty brief—only using a few short sentences.

Okay, let's get to a sample script. Example:

> Hello, my name is Sam. I'm with Rocket Fuel Jingles. Did I catch you at an okay time? Great. Rocket Fuel is a music production company that makes jingles for marketing. My job is to help businesses brand themselves with jingles. What are your thoughts on using a jingle for your advertising?

Okay, so let's discuss what just happened.

First, the script started with your name and the name of your company. By doing this, you establish two identities—yours and your company's. When you do this, you automatically give structure to your business. The person you're speaking with understands that you represent an entity—a real business. With these few words, you've already started to build credibility. If, on the other hand, you called and said, "Hi. This is Jake. I totally rock jingles," you may start to lose ground and trust very quickly with the people you are phoning.

Please understand that doing business in the real world has a lot to do with perception—how you appear will have a direct impact on what kind of money you make. For example, how would you feel about being at a restaurant and paying $50 for an entrée that was served on paper plates? It could be argued that the food is just fine, but there's something to be said about how things are presented. So, make an effort on your presentation.

Next in our script, you asked whether the person had time to speak. By doing this, you are communicating that the people you're calling are esteemed and that their time is precious.

Nothing says "I'm a selfish jerk" like someone who calls and ramrods his or her way into a conversation without ever considering that a person on the phone may not have time to speak at length. If you do this, busy people you call will shut you down right away or be detached, as their mind drifts back to what they were previously doing.

To cultivate a positive experience, just ask whether the person has a moment.

With the aforementioned in mind, I'd like to offer a contingency plan.

Let's say the person you called says, "No, I was just headed off to a meeting . . . can't talk now." Your automatic reflex to this reply should be, "Sorry about that. When is a better time to speak?" If the person tells you when to call back, you've just earned yourself something valuable—words you can use later. You see, when you phone back at the time *this person* indicated, you'd start off the subsequent call by saying something like, "Hi, this is Jake. *You* told me to call you back today. Is this a better time?" Can you see what's happening here? The reason for your callback is now shifting to something the other party is participating in. Your calls will feel less intrusive when you understand that you've been given an official invitation to revisit.

You can even earn super-extra points if the person you are calling is busy every time you call back—so long as *you have been told* to do so. Do you know why? It is my experience that people start to feel bad for standing you up on multiple occasions. At a certain point, they begin to feel it is their duty to *make it up to you*. So, when you finally have your conversation, you will most likely find yourself speaking to people who do not have a whole bunch of verbal defenses ready for you. On the contrary, they are more likely to be agreeable, as their treatment of you has been unfair.

If your person of interest keeps offering you times to call back, make sure you keep following up.

So, let's get back to where we were in the script.

In the next section of your script, you will provide a superfast synopsis of your company and an ultraquick overview of what you offer. I'm emphasizing brevity here because some people have a tendency to drone on and on about themselves or what they've done so as to impress others. Avoid the babble; don't call people and dump a dictionary's worth of words on them, thinking you will impress your listeners. The primary goal here is to position yourself in such a way that each person you've called is willing to have a normal, two-way conversation about your services.

Finally, your introductory script will end with an *open-ended question*.

Open-ended questions are those that begin with the following words: *what, how, why, where, who*, and *when*.

The beauty of open-ended questions is that they promote or *open up* discussion. When you start a question with one of these magical words, the other party is compelled to provide more than a one-word or yes-no answer. Here are a few examples:

- *What* do you know about jingles?
- *How* have you spread the word about your business?
- *Why* do you think jingles are used by major corporations?
- *Where* do you think your slogan will fit in the jingle?
- *Who* makes the marketing decisions for your company?
- *When* can we speak again?

As you seek to keep the conversation going, nothing will be more instrumental than the impact of an open-ended question.

So, there you are, following my instructions, and you arrive at the end of your brief script. You've just asked an open-ended question, but now what?

I invite you to do something revolutionary: *shut up*!

Please don't take offense to being told to shut up; it's for your own good. Seriously! When you close your mouth, you place yourself into a very important position—a position to *listen*!

Listening—The Lost Art

Once you've launched your open-ended question, it's time for you to start listening—I mean, really pay attention. You see, it is at this point that the cogs for your money machine can begin to turn.

So, you've called a company, you've gone through your script; what do you hear?

Is the other person busy or rushing into a meeting? Have you contacted the right individual? Is the person on the other end inviting you to continue on in dialogue or completely shutting you down? Does he or she seem agitated or really welcoming? Failing to pay attention to what the person on the other end is saying—and how it is said—will quickly move you to annoying status; don't be that guy. Pay attention to what's going on so you can make course corrections during your conversation.

Imagine a patron going to a restaurant and having a server whip out a huge list of seafood specials. The customer tries to interrupt the server, but no, the waiter is caught up in pointing out the special—the catch of the day. After repeated attempts to slow the server down, the frustrated diner gives up and allows the restaurant worker to finish. When it's all said and done, the customer finally has a chance to say, "Uh, I'm allergic to fish." This huge waste of time and frustration could have been alleviated by an attentive server.

The point of my example is to point out that a major part of your introduction and initial conversation with any prospect must include dedicated places for you to get feedback from the person with which you are engaging. Listening will inform you how to proceed with potential customers, if at all. If you skip this step, guess what? You're going to get it wrong . . . a lot.

A long time ago, a sales trainer once said to me, "Selling is *not* telling." If you are to be successful selling anything, in this case jingles, it's going to require that you know what's important to your potential customers. That can only happen when you *hear* what's important to them—not blabbing the whole time.

> Your script is a lot like the key to your car; it helps you get things started, but you have to make sensible choices about where you go afterward. Active listening will inform your next move.

As you listen to the person on the call, you will begin to pick up on key information. In fact, what you hear may inspire more questions. You see, skillfully constructed follow-up questions can uncover hidden opportunities. The more you can get someone talking, the more chances you have to find an open door for your jingle company. So, it will be vital for you to ask the *right* questions. Being able to ask the right questions at the right time will help you to move the conversation in the right direction. You'll feel like some sort of Jedi Master conversationalist, mysteriously guiding conversations in a direction that's favorable to you.

You want to see the power of questions in action? Observe lawyers in court. When they ask a question, they don't randomly say things; they already know how they want the story to pan out before a witness ever takes the stand. As a result, all of their questions will lead down a path *the lawyers* see as beneficial.

Let's say you call a company about a jingle and you're told, "No, thank you. Jingles are cheesy. That is not our company's style." Hearing words like this, most callers will hang up the phone and scurry away. In response to this rejection, what if you were to say, "I can understand what you mean about cheesy jingles; I'm not a big fan of them, either. That's why I produce jingles that kind of sound like real, Grammy-nominated songs. Let me have your e-mail address so I can send you a few examples and let you make your decision once you've heard what I can do. What is your e-mail address, please?"

With my previous example, you would be able to take a negative situation and use a strategic question to move things back to where you have a chance to keep the dialogue alive. You may not be able to control the other party, but with the use of proper questions, you can give yourself a fighting chance of survival.

15

BRING THE PARTY TO YOU

Thus far, I have strongly encouraged you to pick up the phone and reach out to potential customers. Although it's the best way to take control of your destiny, it's not the only way to get clients.

Throughout this book, you'll hear me say *a customer contacted me* about getting a jingle made. Sure, I have made it a practice to actively reach out to businesses about my jingle services, but I also *receive* calls from those looking for my services. Why and how are all of these people contacting me? Excellent question; I'm glad you asked.

Online 24/7

The secret to getting people to call me can be found online. The vast majority of customer-initiated conversations have come from my *website.*

In the "Should-Haves" chapter of this book, I talked about how having a jingle-based web page is equivalent to a 24/7 sales force, working on behalf of your music business. While you're hustling at your day job, asleep, or hanging out with friends, a dedicated website could be helping you find new clients—or, rather, helping them find you.

Just yesterday I got a call from a local heating and cooling company, looking to get a jingle made for its business. The awesome part about this company's reaching out to me is it was *already* interested! The caller indicated that the firm would be launching a lot of local radio and TV ads and wanted to get a jingle very soon. That meant the likelihood of my getting the assignment was pretty high. I just had to demonstrate that I know what I'm talking about and can do the job.

Over the years, my website has been one of the most prized tools I've used for my business. Having a website will serve you well, too. Look, technology isn't going anywhere, so maybe it is time you allowed it to work for you!

When discussing websites, I don't want to give you the impression that if you have one, then people will magically call you. Some technical things must be in place for this strategy to work for you. If your eyes are already starting to glaze over, I want you to stick with me here. For tech novices, website development used to be cumbersome, complicated, and incredibly expensive. But nowadays, there are places online that allow you to build a site with nearly the same ease as drafting an e-mail. So, don't get fixated on the "I can't" mentality—you can! Another word of encouragement for the less-than-tech-savvy: your website does not have to be some multipage, technological monstrosity. Rather, it can be a simple, one-page site containing some important yet simple information.

You've taken the time to learn about the jingle business; surely you can take the time to learn about creating a basic website.

So, let's hit the fast-forward button and assume you've taken my advice about creating a web page. I now want to offer a few ideas as to how you can put your web page to work for you.

SEO

Where do you think most people go when they are searching for something online? If you guessed Google, you'd be correct. For the last decade, Google has utterly dominated the "search" world, despite the advent of social media and the presence of competing such search engines as Bing and Yahoo! Google has managed to attract millions and millions of users to its searches daily. Wouldn't it be great if a customer who wanted a jingle could search Google, type in a word or two, and see the name of your company just pop up on the first page? Achieving such a result is done by *search engine optimization*, or SEO for short.

SEO is a technical discipline that requires you to craft your site's syntax and content in a way that will signal Google to display your website on the first few pages of searches related to specific terms, or *keywords*. Google determines where you appear in searches based on something called an algorithm—a complicated software equation that accounts for many relevant factors.

Over the years, people have tried to decode this algorithm and use it to their advantage. However, betting on how to exploit or *game* Google's algorithm is similar to betting in Vegas . . . you'd be wasting your money and time. Instead, you simply need to abide by what Google itself has outlined as best practices for SEO. By simply typing "Google SEO guide"' into the search box, you'll have clear steps for moving your site up in the search results.

Make no mistake: SEO is no walk in the park. As you can tell, this topic can get pretty involved. For that reason, I won't go much further into the technical aspects of it. I bring up the topic of SEO to say that it is something you will have to embrace if you want your website to begin to bring customers to you.

Fortunately, you can begin to learn and implement some of the basics by watching a few online tutorials. No, you may not become an SEO virtuoso by doing so, but you can learn enough to give your site more visibility.

As you look into this topic, try starting with the following areas: *link building*, *page descriptions*, *header tags*, and *duplicate content removal.*

If the SEO thing is still giving you the sensation of a slushy-brain-freeze and you'd rather have someone else do it for you, I offer a word of caution: a ton of SEO companies out there promise to make you number one on Google. I strongly recommend you be highly suspicious of these claims. The vast majority of offers I've seen are total garbage. A lot of these SEO operations are people working in the shadows, looking to rip you off. For those that happen to be legitimate, their services will come at a very high price. I implore you to learn what you can about this area yourself so the proverbial wool is never pulled over your eyes.

SEM

I've done my best to emphasize that not all the things I'm instructing you to do in this book are a walk in the park. Some of these things can be downright challenging. Learning SEO happens to be one of them. Even when you learn a few things about optimizing your site, the results, for a variety of reasons, are not always immediate. And I understand that sometimes you just want to get out there and make things happen a little faster.

Is some sort of shortcut available? The answer is yes. It's called SEM, or search engine marketing. You may also hear this called *paid searches.*

Similar to SEO, SEM involves you being found online when people are looking for, in our case, jingles. The thing is, being found online in this way *costs money.*

Every time you visit Google and search, what pops up at the very top of the page and to the right? Google shows *paid* search results followed by organic (unpaid) results. These highly visible search links are search engine marketing at work.

The beauty of SEM is that it allows you to bypass the technical and time-eating mazes of SEO, and blasts you right to the front of the line on Google (or Bing or Yahoo!, for that matter).

Although SEM with Google, Bing, or Yahoo! is a great way to establish quick visibility for your website, know that you need to be aware of some pitfalls.

In the earlier years of my business, I dumped a lot of money into SEM. The main reason for doing so was because I did not appear in the search results. If, for example, someone were to type "where to buy a jingle" in Google, my site would most likely *not* have shown, as I had yet to achieve the accomplishments necessary to appear in the search engines organically. Besides, search engine advertising seemed to be a pretty reasonable proposition, as I only paid Google a few cents when a potential customer clicked on my website. This is known as CPC, or cost-per-click, which means you're charged only when someone engages your listing.

When I first started my SEM campaign, it was an amazing success. I was getting phone calls and e-mails from people left and right. As time went on, things started to slow substantially; I couldn't figure out what was going on. As I did a little poking around, I noticed a few things: I saw the steady glut of competitors coming into the jingle world, sucking clients away from my business. As other jingle companies came to the SEM world, they drove up the cost to advertise. You see, CPC ads are auction based—the highest bid wins. Finally, I noticed that some people were clicking my links but never contacting me. This meant I was paying for online activity but not seeing a payoff. In retrospect, I learned these particular clicks were a result of curious people looking to work in the jingle business. Also, some of these clicks erroneously came from those looking for a closely related search term, such as "jingle bell rock." No matter what the reason, I was no longer seeing the results I wanted.

The previous account should serve as a warning. Using SEM to get your site in front of customers doesn't work like magic. A learning curve is involved with SEM as well. There are a myriad of settings, parameters, dos, and don'ts you need to figure out to be successful. You've heard me say that a few online videos will do you some good; this is no different. Take the time to learn how SEM works. Failing to do so will cause you to spend a lot of money on a strategy that is not firing on all cylinders.

Social Media

Thus far, I've placed an emphasis on being found on Google.

Please don't misunderstand; I don't own any stock in the company. My recommendation to consider them is due to the size of its customer base and reach. There are, however, many other ways to advertise online. One major way is through social media.

Understand that marketing with social media should be seen as an indirect means of advertising. To put it another way, social media marketing is about building relationships. After these connections are forged, you will have the liberty to ask people to consider buying your product.

Think about your own experiences. How do you feel about hopping on Instagram, Facebook, and Twitter and being hit with a ton of buy-me messages: apps, shoes, supplements? You start to feel that it's too much, right?

If you want to have success marketing your jingles on a social platform, I offer this salient piece of advice: be sure to give and not take. In other words, your social media posts concerning your jingle business should offer people such things as fun facts, helpful tips, expert advice, and even comical contributions. When you do this, you are actually *giving* people something to look at—and maybe even showing off your sense of creativity. As you engage in this fashion, people in these places will regard you as a trusted resource rather than as some spammy predator. In short, you'd be taken seriously.

You could, for instance, create a series of video blogs. In these clips, you could swap music in and out of existing commercials—prompting your subscribers to think about how the overall mood of the ad changes, depending on the music. You could take this idea even further and interject some humor. You could develop a series of videos that feature a number of music ad mismatches; e.g. mashing kazoo music up with funeral home ads. Once the fun is over, you'd wrap up your clip with a small endorsement for your jingle company. As we discussed in our "No Copying" chapter, avoid *using or copying* someone else's work without authorization. As a solution, check out such sites as Vimeo. Search for commercial clips that allow free use and changes. You're looking for videos with the following Creative Commons licenses: Public Domain (CC0), Attribution Alone (BY), or Attribution + ShareAlike (BY-SA).

Social media gives you a forum where you can reach a huge amount of people. Just be sure you're aware of its delicate give-and-take balance, and you'll get the attention you need to sell your jingles.

E-mail

The previous methods may seem a bit out of reach for some due to cost or complexity; I get it. If that describes you, there's always e-mail! It's easy, free, and (hopefully by now) familiar. If used properly, e-mail can be a powerful way to make an impression on potential customers. But note I said, "If used properly"!

The world of e-mail marketing can be summed up in two categories: spammy nuisances or informative communications. Your aim is to be in the second camp—providing great content that encourages businesses to interact with you.

Think about it; e-mail can bring together several of the powerful tools I talked about before. You can attach a *brochure*. E-mail allows you to link back to your *website*. You are able to attach or link to *samples/demos* of your work.

Just last week, I got a call from a GSM at a Knoxville radio station. As depicted earlier, he was interested in having his account executives use jingles to draw new advertisers to his station. As it turned out, I sent an e-mail to about two hundred radio salespeople that day. This gentleman happened to see it and responded. One out of two hundred is not a huge ratio, but if that one winds up doing business with me, I stand to make a few thousand bucks. I like those odds.

I highly recommend searching for free e-mail marketing services online. Such services as VerticalResponse, MailChimp, and others offer free ways of constructing, sending, and tracking e-mails. Many of these services offer a bunch of tools that will help you be far more effective at managing your efforts than, let's say, using your Yahoo! account. Plus, these services institute safeguards so your e-mail campaigns do not get flagged immediately as spam.

Find a Referrer

Another way of getting customers to call you is to locate someone who will refer you to other businesses.

A while back, an account executive at a radio station contacted me because he was working with a car dealer who'd asked him about getting a jingle made. Since his station did not provide this service in-house, he wound up contacting me. When we spoke, he asked whether I would be willing to give him a small cut of the money I was to collect from the dealership—a commission, of sorts. Initially, I was taken aback by his audacious request, but the more I thought about it, the more I saw the sense in complying. I ended up giving the salesman about $400 from a $2,750 deal. I thought about it this way: I would have never been introduced to the car dealer if it hadn't been for the radio sales guy. I felt it was a fair trade-off.

After this deal was complete, do you know what happened next? The same salesman got motivated by the cash I gave him. He began to actively look for others who might be open to the idea of a jingle. He, on his own, volunteered to become a salesman for *my* company due to the incentive he got. Due to the fact that I had an ongoing business relationship with him, the companies he brought to me were already confident in my abilities. His referrals alone netted me well over $15,000! I didn't have to advertise to make this money. The opportunities just showed up based on *his* efforts. He acted as a referrer, essentially talking me up before I ever got an introduction with the business—a perfect scenario.

Given my example, I don't want you to be confused. In the "Who Will Buy Your Jingles?" chapter, I mentioned that AEs may help connect you with businesses. However, the vast majority of them are *not* looking for you to cut them in on the financial action. In fact, some stations prohibit this. It just so happens that the sales guy I used in my example was permitted by his employer to do so. If you ever come across such an instance, it's wise to ask your referrer about his or her company policies, as to not place your helper in jeopardy.

Finding someone who can act as a *referrer* for you may take some time; however, when you find someone willing to promote or refer your business, it will be your key to making money without a lot of hassle.

As you seek out a referrer, look for someone who has a lot of dealings with business owners. Here are a few people who could make great referrers:

- Voice-over professionals
- Broadcast salespeople (radio, TV, cable)
- Videographer/photographer/web designer
- People at a local chamber of commerce
- People at local networking groups

As you look for these people, it may make good business sense to incentivize the efforts of your referring partner. In other words, *give the referrer money*! A few crisp bills will do wonders for spreading the name of your business. However, I recommend that you compensate such people *only* when their recommendation leads to a paying customer!

16

WHAT TO CHARGE

Now let's get to the burning question that you've been itching to ask me: *How much to charge for a jingle?*

I'll get to jingle pricing in a moment. Before I do, let me ask you a question: *How much does a house cost?* If we're pushed into a corner and forced to provide some sort of answer, you and I would both likely start off by saying, "Well, it depends . . . " Jingle prices, like house prices, depend on a number of factors: how eager is the seller, how eager is the buyer, how are competitors pricing things, what is the geographical location, who made it, what were the costs for producing it, and so on. Understand that I'm not trying to avoid answering the question of how to price your jingle. Just know there are a lot of variables that may change what you ultimately decide as the price structure for your recording services.

Let's jump into the things that will affect your rates the most.

Geography

Where your jingle is to be used will greatly impact how you price it. This widely accepted norm is the main driving force behind pricing your jingles in accordance with *geographic usage.*

The rationale behind charging according to geography is pretty simple. Certain places have more residents; the more people your music touches, the more you should be paid.

If, for example, a jingle is to be used in one small town in Montana, you'd have a low price for that. If, on the other hand, a company desires to blanket the Eastern Seaboard with your jingle, you'd request a much higher rate.

To make things simple, I recommend developing prices for three geographic tiers: *local*, *regional*, and *national*

Before moving on, let me clarify a point. When I talk about geographic usage, I'm referring to a jingle's being aired via, radio, TV, or cable. In just a moment we will get to online pricing. For now, understand that the Internet should not be factored into geography, given its global footprint.

LOCAL USE

Local use can be defined as *one* metropolitan area or media market (known as DMA in TV and TSA/MSA in radio). You can also use distance as a demarcation. For instance, *local* can be defined as anywhere within a 50-mile radius of an establishment or of the center of the main city/town.

There are times when it will make good business sense to move your prices either above or below the local price range I am about to suggest. This action is recommended when your jingle is to be utilized in a single yet large metropolitan area. On the flip side, prices may need to go down if we're dealing with a very tiny town—far away from any major city.

Metropolitan area centers in the United States are assigned a number, or *rank*. In the media world, the rank of any given city is determined by how many people reside in that area. The larger the population, the lower the rank. The smaller the population, the higher the rank.

So, why does the size or rank of a city matter when pricing jingles? It's all about being paid for the number of people your jingle reaches.

For instance, New York City is ranked number 1 in the country. Dubuque, Iowa, is ranked 517. So, when a sixty-second radio commercial airs in New York City, it potentially can reach over 16 million people. An identical ad in Dubuque would only have a maximum reach of 144,000 audience members. Given this reality, should the cost for the ad be the same in both places? The answer is no. In a population-dense city, the cost of the ad can be astronomical, whereas the small city's prices can be supercheap. It's basic economics, so just go with it.

Having said all of this, I'd recommend *starting* your local use price range at $3,500 for cities ranked between 1 and 20. Cities with a ranking of 21 to 149 can be priced from $2,000 to $3,500. If you are dealing with businesses in smaller markets, such as cities ranked 150 and up, it may make sense to lock your price range between $500 and $2,000.

REGIONAL USE

Regional use can be defined as statewide use, in most instances.

If the business borders another state and airs commercials in adjacent media markets, regional use may encompass multiple markets. Have you ever heard of places in the country described as the Tri-State Area?

The same can be true of companies that may advertise in a handful of nonadjacent media markets in other parts of the country. For instance, this would be true for a dry cleaner that has locations in three cities: Indianapolis, Cincinnati, and Detroit.

Regional use would also make sense for a company that wishes to air their jingle in a group of smaller states, such as those in New England.

NATIONAL USE

National use should be pretty clear at this point. Any company that wishes to use your jingle in a nationwide media push should fall into this category.

National usage does not assume that the company is in every single city and state. It simply implies that the broadcast marketing reach of the company is quite substantial. For instance, if a company has two hundred locations spread throughout twenty-five states, I'd consider that national use.

Now let's outline price ranges:

Geographic Use	Price Range
Local (small town)	$500-$2000
Local	$1500-$3500
Regional	$3500-$10,000
National	$10,000 and up

By now you may have noticed there are some pretty wide ranges for the pricing tiers, right? Well, the distance between the bottom end of a range and the top can be attributed to a lot of factors. Let's tackle some of the most prominent things.

Your Value

For the sake of this topic, I'd like to introduce you to a term called *price point*. View price point as the value category a product or service fits into. These levels could be, for example: budget, standard, premium, or elite. If it'll help, think: Hyundai, Chevy, Honda, or Mercedes.

I'm introducing this term now because we need to see where your business is on the totem pole, so to speak. In other words, the value of what you offer will dictate average costs for your jingles.

Are you a budget, standard, premium, or elite jingle provider? This fact will dictate how far up or down you'll find yourself on any given price tier. If you're just getting started, with no resume and having basic equipment, you may not be able to convince anyone to shell out $3,500 for a local-use jingle. If, however, you have a verifiable track record in the music biz and work out of a professional studio, you may be able to command premium dollars.

If you are operating on the lower end of the spectrum, don't let that discourage you. You can still make a lot of money right there in your basement. And if you recall, I started at the bottom—living in a tiny apartment, recording music out of what was then my two-year-old's bedroom.

Despite my encouragement, you may totally reject the idea that you're anything less than a high-end jingle producer. I get it; cockiness is the musician's Achilles' heel. However, if you don't rein in this part of your character, you'll kill your business before it ever starts. You'll be out there demanding that businesses pay a billion dollars for your jingles, just because *you* crowned yourself beyond-great. In the end, companies will be dismissive; you'll burn bridges, and make zero dinero.

Although you can opt to charge whatever you want (it's your company, after all), create a pricing strategy in line with your capabilities—not solely according to what you *want* to earn. In other words, your price point should be realistic. To help you with that, I will soon provide some actual prices I've charged and have seen from other jingle companies.

Jingle Content

Another factor that determines price is what your jingle comprises. How involved is the music-making process?

If your client wants a coffeehouse sound, such as a basic lead vocal and acoustic guitar, you may opt to be on the lower end of the pricing scale. If, however, your client is asking for a real piccolo, cellist, and full brass section, that changes things . . . a lot! I look at it this way: If I have to get a lot of outside musicians and singers to participate in the recording process, I charge more. After all, I have to pay these participants. This will also be true if your client is demanding a specific contributing musician. Earlier I mentioned that one of my clients insisted on having a vocalist who sounded similar to country singer George Strait. I held audition after audition. I can tell you, firsthand, it took forever to find a guy who was convincing enough.

If finding your project talent equates to diving through haystacks to find a needle, I'd suggest adjusting your quote to match the workload and potential headache.

Complexity

As you build your customer base, you'll come across supersimple requests, average requests, and nearly impossible musical feats. Move yourself along the pricing scale to match the project.

If a client comes to the table, describing exactly what it wants—even already having the words and melody, you may opt to lower your price a bit. On the opposite side of things, you may be asked for a totally original, one-minute Broadway-inspired jingle, packed with tons of words, messaging, and instrumentation that all has to flow seamlessly.

With complex requests like the latter, way too much can go wrong. There's an increased likelihood you're in for a lengthy creative slug-fest with a customer—going back and forth on details. In these cases, start with a higher price tag so you compensate yourself accordingly for the anticipated time required.

The Law of Averages

As discussed, you will have to set your prices based on some of the previously outlined factors. When you do, there may be a need to adjust up or down based on the type of feedback you are getting from customers. After some time, you will settle on a reasonable price point.

Despite all of this, I bet you are still looking for me just to tell you what to charge, right? I still can't do that for you, but I can fill you in on what I and others are likely to charge for a jingle.

As I outline what I deem to be average jingle prices, know that these rates presuppose we are dealing with a typical recording—nothing too extensive, nor anything skimpy. Also know that the prices include a few extra cuts/edits along with the main or full-sing version of the jingle.

Geographic Use	Average Price
Local (small town)	$1500
Local	$3000
Regional	$4500
National	$12,000

If you were to slap one of these price tags on your jingle, most people will not bat an eye *if* your work is comparable to other jingle companies. If you feel your work measures up, these rates should offer some guidance as to where to begin.

ONLINE JINGLE PRICES

Let's now venture into uncharted territory . . . the Internet.

I've been able to provide pretty solid figures for what to charge for jingles when they are to be used on TV or radio. That's because geographic considerations make it fairly easy to dial in a price based on the number of people in any given city. On the web, the reach is literally global—billions of potential audience members. If we were to apply the same price calculations here, no one would be able to afford a jingle for, say, a YouTube ad.

When it comes to assigning a price tag for a jingle to be used only on the web, I defer to the company's size as the primary determinant. If the company itself is pretty small and also seems to have a tiny online footprint, I'd charge local use rates. If the company is midsize and has a strong online presence, I'd use regional rates. If the company happens to be, say, Amazon, I'd use national pricing for its jingle quote.

I remember getting a call from a home builder in the Washington, DC, area who was beginning to sell eco-friendly, green homes. It wanted to promote its housing development with a few videos on its website—no radio, no TV. Given the builder's local presence and size, I ended up charging $2,800 for the jingle package. I felt this was a pretty good rate, though I didn't have a lot of comparative data to back up my conclusion.

Although web advertising is no longer a new concept, a widely accepted online price structure for jingles has yet to be discovered. As a result, take the aforementioned price tips and be ready to negotiate.

SATELLITE RADIO

From what I've experienced, satellite radio is the unkempt little brother of the Internet. In other words, you may find yourself in a similar pricing conundrum—struggling to find a clear way to value your services with this type of medium. Satellite, much like online advertising, has a pretty massive reach. However, affordability will most often be a function of the size and scope of the company looking to advertise, not geography. Although smaller companies have national reach with satellite, they may only have a marketing budget of a few thousand dollars. Therefore, shelling out ten thousand bucks for a jingle may seem outrageous to a smaller enterprise. Your prices will have to shift based on who your client is.

Slippery Slope?

All this in mind, randomly sliding prices around can have you slipping down a morally reprehensible slope quite quickly. In fact, you'd be breaking laws in some places if you were to just arbitrarily change your prices on a whim.

With that said, this is *not* the mind-set I'm advocating for concerning online and satellite radio.

A company's size and reach is a valid reason to adjust your prices with respect to Internet and satellite advertising. This is because you should be compensated in accordance with the number of people your work can potentially reach. And since geography is off the table for the key indicator, we'll now focus on music *use*.

For example, McDonald's will get more use out of your music online and with satellite, as compared to Mike's Custom Deer Stands. That's because the sheer number of ads McDonald's airs is likely to be exponentially higher than those of a small firm. It's not about gouging the fast-food giant because *it can afford it.* Rather, it's about being compensated for music material's impacting and influencing a huge audience.

Are You a Sellout?

In the contract section, I began to talk about the rights you provide to your customer. Given what we've covered thus far, know that we are talking about copyrights. Keep in mind that one of the most critical clauses you'll address with a customer will surround subject of ownership. *Who* ends up with full rights to the jingle can greatly impact what you may ultimately decide to charge.

In the music marketing world, selling jingles will usually take you down one of two roads: *one-time fee* or *work-for-hire.* Licensing is a third, rare option we'll discuss momentarily.

A *one-time fee* is a scenario whereby you agree to loan your copyrighted material to a business indefinitely. As the name suggests, you are to receive a one-time payment for such use.

A *work-for-hire* agreement is a provision that requires you hand over all your copyright privileges and ownership to the client. This is also known as a *buyout.* If you agree to a buyout, understand that you are selling *all* your rights. Once the jingle leaves your studio, you have zero say in how your music is to be used or what for; your customer owns it outright.

Which path should you take? How should your choice affect the final price?

Let's take a look . . .

One-Time Fee

Given my years and experience in the business, I feel it is to your benefit to retain your rights for any music you make.

This philosophy should permeate all your creative endeavors.

How many broke, one-hit-wonder artists have you seen throughout the years? Many of them are down and out because they never had any real ownership in their work; their labels, producers, publishers, and songwriters have all the equity.

For some reason, many jingle writers suffer from the same pathology—getting cash, but never retaining a stake in anything. So, in light of my soapbox stump speech, it should come as no surprise that I'm pushing you to *pursue one-time-fee deals* with your clients, which means making cash while retaining your copyrights. If you choose this path, you're safe sticking with the price models I've outlined.

Why am I making such a big deal out of a jingle you are being paid *once* for? In a word, it's control. Retaining the rights to your jingle insulates you from customer reprisal, provides protection against being taken advantage of, and you also gain control over potential future earnings.

CUSTOMER REPRISAL

I keep the rights to my jingles to avoid any potential copyright quarrels with my clients.

Imagine that you create a country-themed jingle for a client. Let's say your contract states that you agree to give all your rights to your client. After finishing up the final draft of the jingle, the customer is happy and agrees to pay, and you skip off into the sunset. A year later, the same customer calls to tell you that you are infringing on *its* copyright. How is that possible? You are informed that the jingle that *you* created for this company sounds exactly like a new jingle *you* since created for another client you recently acquired. The customer you initially sold your rights to demands you remove your sound-alike jingle from the airwaves because it mirrors something it now owns.

Is it plausible for you to end up fighting such a battle? I can't say with certainty. But why leave a door open for potential problems?

UNSAVORY MIDDLEMAN

Retaining your rights under a one-time fee agreement can protect you against those who want to take advantage of you.

There may be instances where someone offers to pay you a low amount for a jingle, but insists on full rights. These types of situations have always caused me to pause.

Let's say you're superdesperate for cash and agree to sell a jingle at a bargain-basement price. What happens if the person or company you sold your work to turns out to be a broker for a huge national company with a massive TV presence? With that knowledge, of course, you would have insisted on a different price structure, given the use of the material, right? But at this point, any say you had in the argument was lost the very moment you gave your rights away. So, if the entity you dealt with decided to repackage or resell your jingle, it can do whatever it wants with it. The kicker is that the customer most likely will slap its name all over the jingle and give you absolutely no creative credit.

Again, you have no recourse at this point.

POTENTIAL FUTURE EARNINGS

Finally, I'd like to cover what can happen further down the road.

When you retain the rights to your creative work *and* impose proper restrictions in your contract, including limiting geographic use, you give yourself the ability to cash in on future use of your jingle *if* the customer asks to move beyond the boundaries of the initial agreement.

Imagine that you sold a jingle for a one-time fee of $2,000 to a small bakery in Nowheresville. For the first year, the company is happy airing its jingle on the local radio stations. However, the success of the bakery has now garnered the attention of some big investors, and as if overnight, this little bakery is now starting to branch out and open locations all over the country. Up until now, the cornerstone of its ads has been, you guessed it, the jingle you made. If you played your cards correctly, *retained your rights*, and restricted the company's use to one town (per my previous advice), you'd be in a position to renegotiate a bigger deal, should this establishment choose to go national with *your* jingle.

Keeping your copyrights is all about protection and more potential earnings. Translation: Strongly consider sticking with one-time fee deals.

Buyout

I've spent all of this time outlining the merits of retaining your rights, so why even go down the other road, the path of a *buyout*?

There may be times when a buyout is more advantageous than sticking with your guns and demanding a one-time-fee arrangement. By "advantageous" I mean you may be put in a place where *not* offering a buyout to a client will cost you the entire deal.

In my years dealing with small business owners, I've come across quite a few owners who have been abject control freaks; many of them have become accustomed to owning everything that serves their interests.

This is not an insult; it's just the DNA that allows these people to be at the top of their game. As a result, you may find that a lot of entrepreneurs will demand that they own your jingle outright. They will potentially see the jingle as an asset—no different than a conference room table.

View things from their perspective for a moment. Wouldn't you feel weirded out if a guy you bought your guitar from three years ago called you up from time to time to check on it because he felt as though he "technically" still owns the guitar? Of course that would feel creepy.

Not knowing how ownership works in the music industry may result in your clients' feeling the same way. It's up to you to educate them on copyright ownership, if you can. If not, you may find yourself without a deal or facing the prospect of feeling forced to accept a buyout.

Whenever I see a buyout coming, I don't get all crazy and indignant with the company I'm speaking with. On the contrary, I get a little giddy. Due to the customer's resistance, I may have just moved myself into a position to earn more than I had previously thought.

You see, I always start the price conversation with the understanding that we are working toward a one-time-fee agreement by using the price brackets outlined earlier. As covered, these rates will provide the customer with usage for its prescribed geographic area. In the event a customer does not want to comply with geographic constraints and/or does not like the idea of my claiming rights to the finished work, I simply *up* the price. Yup, I jack up my rates, just like that! You may be thinking, "Hey, isn't that underhanded?" Nope, not at all. As discussed, I don't change the rates arbitrarily, under the cover of darkness. On the contrary, I choose to have a direct conversation with my client about the price change, letting it know the original prices no longer stand, given *its* insistence of a total buyout.

Conversations with my clients in these instances may go like this:

> Mr. Jones, I'm happy to hear that you'd like to work with our company. However, the $3,000 for your jingle package only covers use within your city. If you don't want such restraints and are seeking a complete buyout, where you own the material outright, that will change our pricing model substantially. The cost for total ownership in a jingle package with these conditions is . . .

At this point, you may be asking a familiar question: "How much do I charge?" In all my years in this business, I've seen prices all over the place. I've yet to see any norms when it comes to jingle buyouts. As a result, my advice will come straight from my experiences.

When asked to provide a buyout, I recommend a *50 to 100 percent price increase.*

If, for example, you quote a local florist $2,000 and it insists on a buyout, ask for $3,000 to $4,000. If the customer starts to give you a hard time about these higher rates, politely remind the client that the original one-time-fee option is still available, along with restrictions, of course.

Licensing

Before we finish up on the subject of prices, I'd like to talk about a wild card—licensing.

When one licenses music, it provides the creator (licensor) the ability to *rent out* creative content to customers—kind of like a car rental. As long as the customer holds the keys, it's paying.

This is an attractive path because it provides the possibility of a consistent paycheck—residual income from your music! Although the prospect of skipping down to the bank on a regular basis sounds great to *you*, many businesses don't feel the same way. You're likely to find that the vast majority of customers you deal with simply want to pay a one-time fee and move on. For small businesses, it's a simple and clean transaction. For that reason, licensing jingles is a tough road to travel, especially on the lower end of the price spectrum.

However, things tend to change when discussing licensing music to large advertising agencies.

Understand that huge agencies have many guidelines and rules dictating how they operate. Many of these parameters are dictated by the caliber of companies they represent. No agency at the upper echelon wants to be found ripping off contractors on behalf of its clients. Could you imagine the blowback Walmart or Apple would receive if it was determined that people creating or appearing in its commercials were being paid peanuts? It would be a nightmare. As a result, agencies will follow these practices: hiring union actors, paying scale (standardized remuneration for a job assignment), and, in our case, licensing music at a fair rate.

I know I just finished telling you large agencies, as opposed to smaller ones, are likely to license your jingles, but I don't want to offer too much guidance as to how to price your jingles for them. After all, I've already stated that you most likely will see figures exceeding $10,000. With that said, just know large agencies tend to have clearly defined budgets for music. From what I've seen, these budgets are usually on a take-it-or-leave-it basis. The good news is you're not likely to *leave it.* That's because of the reasons I stated earlier: large agencies go through a lot of *i*-dotting, and *t*-crossing with vendors. This will most likely result in a paycheck that far exceeds your financial expectations. *The vast majority of these licensing deals should bring you north of five figures.* I can't, however, say how far north. That's because the terms *territory* and *medium* will inform how much pay is involved.

What do these terms mean? Let's go further into this.

Medium: When you are creating jingles for agencies, or anyone for that matter, you need to know *where* your music will appear. The place in which your jingle appears is the medium, such as TV, radio, online, cable, DVD, and so on. The budget for the jingle package will vary, depending on where it is to appear. For instance, a jingle designed for a TV ad most likely will have a far higher payout than a jingle designed for a YouTube promotion. If the agency asks to use the jingle in multiple places, the budget should be even higher.

Term: How long can the agency use the material you created? The length of time is known as the *term.* I've seen situations where an agency may only want to purchase the use of a tune for just a few weeks—maybe for a seasonal promotion. There are other times when agencies are seeking open-ended usage of your music. This is known as *perpetuity*, by the way. As you would imagine, the longer the term, the more likely you are to see more cash. Keep this in mind should you get into negotiations over price.

Territory: Having a jingle featured in one city is one thing; airing your jingle nationally is another. The geographic location your jingle covers is the *territory*—a huge determinant for how much you're paid. Before embarking on any jingle project, you and the agency should have this topic front and center. Local jingles are priced in the thousands, whereas national jingles should be priced in the five-figure-and-beyond category.

Although other terms will come up in the course of a conversation with an agency, the aforementioned points are those that will have the most significant impact on the potential money involved.

The beauty of licensing music with agencies is that they will often want to relicense the same work and potentially offer you even more to do so. That's because the more a jingle is used, the more powerful it becomes.

Besides all of this, having your jingle featured with a huge national brand is a prestige win. Your credibility will skyrocket once you are able to associate your music production skills with a renowned business.

Price Deathtrap

As I wrap up this chapter, I'd be remiss if I did not talk about the elephant in the room: those that sell jingles for next to nothing.

Whether it be Fiverr or some other ultracheap alternative, you will likely face a situation where what you're asking to be paid far exceeds that of someone else. This unfortunate reality comes with the competitive-territory you're looking to thrive in.

Should you find yourself in a position where a customer is berating you for how high your prices are, I'd encourage you to be open to knocking off a few hundred bucks from the quote, if warranted. But if the customer is comparing you to some low-ball jingle maker it's found online, *do not* cheapen yourself by offering some crazy 90 percent–off deal just to remain competitive.

Do not slash your prices to compete with extremely low rates.

A former business partner and friend of mine, named Ron, runs a studio across town. He was recently contacted by one of his longtime clients, who was pretty mad. The customer began to tell my buddy that the cost of his recording services was way too high and that he had all but ripped off the company for the services he provides. My friend was astonished. "Why do you suddenly think my prices are too high?" he asked. And there it was. The client had been surfing around on Fiverr and found a guy willing to handle the project for less than ten bucks. My friend's price was nearly $2,000—quite a big difference! Ron, being a smart and confident professional, told his customer, "Go ahead . . ." He began to encourage his client to take the cheap offer found *if* the company was prepared to deal with the type of quality it were likely to get, and *if* it was willing to take a chance on someone who didn't have a fraction of his experience. From one *if* to another, Ron substantiated why he's worth every dime he charges.

What do you think happened after Ron issued this qualifications smack-down? You're right. My friend got the project!

Remember this story! One day you might have to look a customer in the eye and say you're worth every penny. Do it, but be able to back up every word with quality results. Take the time to reread some of the chapters in this book and really get to know this business so the overall value of what you provide will never be compared to anything at the bottom of the barrel.

17

THE CONTRACT

Now that we've covered all the building blocks for selling jingles, you next have to bring things together so you and your client are clear on the expectations of your business relationship. In short, you need a contract.

I said this many times throughout this book and I will restate it now: I am not a lawyer. As we talk about drafting a contract for working with customers, I highly suggest you get the involvement of a legal professional. Laws, as you know, vary from location to location. As a consequence, you need to make sure any contract you draw up can stand up under legal scrutiny.

With all of that said, I'd like to introduce a sample contract that shows you how to pull together some of the things we've covered.

Sample Contract

This Agreement is hereby made on ________________ (date), by and between Your Jingle Company, hereinafter referred to as "Licensor," 555 Main Street. Jammerville, IL USA 60611 and ________________________________, hereinafter referred to as "Licensee."

The product description:

ONE (1) original jingle package, which will include a minimum of SIX (6) time-variations of a single, exclusive commercial music theme

Total cost: $2,750.00

1. "Licensor" hereby grants to "Licensee" unlimited broadcast and nonbroadcast rights (limitless usage within any media form without further permission by "Licensor" or further royalties or payments of any kind to "Licensor") for the period 99 years in the Dallas, Texas MSA/DMA.
2. "Licensee" is hereby granted the right to allow limitless simulcasts, translators, cable TV or satellite transmission or other usage of final draft only. Limitless telephone or cable transmissions via the Internet or e-mail are also permitted, and are not restricted to MSA, DMA, or single metropolitan area.
3. "Licensor" retains all copyrights and ownership of material and/or music at all times. "Licensor" agrees that during and after the expiration of the licensing agreement, the production itself, its melodies and exacting styles may not be additionally reproduced or derivatives made within "Licensee's MSA, DMA or metropolitan area." "Licensor" retains the right to use all material recorded for "Licensee" for demonstration purposes.
4. Renewal for additional terms, periods and areas are at the sole discretion of "Licensor." Upon the expiration of the stated term, "Licensee" will cease and desist the broadcasting or any usage of the described commercial(s) or derivatives thereof.
5. All master files are the sole property of the "Licensor" at all times.
6. "Licensor" agrees to grant immediate use of final draft upon receiving full payment from "Licensee." This contract becomes fully enforceable and legally binding when fully executed, not upon receipt of payment. A 50% deposit will be due in advance per the specifications of attachment "A" or invoice; however, failure to pay does not render the contract unenforceable or invalid. The remaining 50% must be paid in full no later than 90 days from the signing of this agreement.
7. "Licensee" is prohibited from the use, resale and/or dissemination of rejected drafts. Furthermore, "Licensor" shall retain full rights to rejected drafts and may use for other purposes including, but not limited to, other advertisers.
8. "Licensee" is in no way obligated to hire or commission "Licensor" for any additional work in the future. "Licensor" is not responsible

or liable for any adjustments necessary due to the negligence or fault of "Licensee."

9. In the event of default in terms or conditions, "Licensee" agrees that there shall be no broadcast or any usage of the above described product owned by "Licensor" until such breach is remedied. Should broadcast or any promotional usage or copying take place by "Licensee" or its agents, customers or users take place during a default by "Licensee," "Licensee" agrees to be responsible for statutory penalties under the US copyright laws without prior notice to cease and desist. Should default, broadcast or copying of the above described product take place, "Licensee" will pay "Licensor" a fee of $1,000.00 per each broadcast or copying. "Licensee" also agrees to fully pay for all costs "Licensor" may incur for remedying a default, including reasonable attorney's fees.
10. Illinois law shall govern this Agreement.
11. "Licensee" hereby agrees to be bound by a fully executed fax, e-mail, or photocopy of this agreement.
12. The individual signing this license agreement warrants and represents that he or she has the express authority to enter into this agreement and jointly and severally binds the "Licensor" fully herein. This license agreement shall not be binding until fully executed. This document is fully executed when signed by "Licensor" and "Licensee."
13. This is the full and complete agreement. It is acknowledged this agreement may be amended only in writing and signed by authorized agents of "Licensor" and "Licensee." If one or more items are deemed inapplicable, it is agreed that all other parts of this agreement remain in full force.

Now that you've had a chance to review this sample contract, I won't bore you with all the legalese. Get with an attorney to review what constitutes an ironclad agreement. I, on the other hand, would like to cover things unique to our industry.

THE PRODUCT

As you look over the sample contract, you will see a brief description of what is being provided. This is found under the "product description" area near the beginning of the agreement.

Nothing will breed conflict faster than a misunderstanding over what a client thinks it is paying for. Do yourself a favor and be sure a clear description of your jingle is included in your contract, as to lessen any potential problems.

THE PRICE

How much are you getting paid? Leave nothing to chance and clearly outline this in your contract. You were told you could earn thousands of dollars; that's why we started this journey, right? So, don't blow all of your effort on forgetting to add the cost of your services in the contract. In our example, you will find this just below the product description.

RESTRICTIONS

Earlier we talked about pricing your jingles according to certain restrictions—geography being a major one. Sections 1 and 2 of the sample agreement are where area of use is defined for the customer. The aforementioned version of the contract limits the use of the jingle package to the advertiser's city. This language is found at the end of section 1.

OWNERSHIP

Are you retaining your copyrights or signing over everything to your client in a buyout? This is addressed in sections 3, 5, and 7 of the agreement. In this instance, the rights for the jingle have been retained, while affording the customer exclusive usage within its city. The agreement determines that the jingle producer will refrain from producing similar-sounding jingles for competitors in that media market. The contract also states that any/all musical ideas the client rejects belong to the jingle producer to use per his or her discretion.

GET MONEY NOW

There, couched in the middle of the contract, is section 6. I happen to believe this section is incredibly important to the entire process. This section deals with getting money up front, like, right now!

Did I surprise you with this one? Okay, let's take a step back and cover a few things.

When you operate a small business and are offering a service with a relatively big price tag, it's not uncommon to ask for the buyer to "put some money down." This is especially true in creative circles.

I never start jingle projects without first asking for a *50% deposit.* Sure, doing this can feel a bit forward, but it's the norm in the industry. As a result, you shouldn't feel weirded out by the prospect of collecting money before scoring one note.

Requiring a deposit will also serve as a "trust fall" exercise for your customer. This request will quickly notify you of potential danger down the road. If, for example, a client refuses to make a deposit, it simply may not trust you. As a consequence, you need to do what you can to garner trust—dig up references, send more samples, or whatever it will take to make that customer feel more comfortable. Unchecked mistrust will eventually serve to undermine your credibility at some point. Deal with it now.

Collect 50 percent of your money upfront.

If a client is unwilling to make a deposit, it could be a sign that it will flake on you later. Look, when a customer puts its money where its mouth is, things get "real"; deposits are indicative of how serious (or not serious) your client may be.

I once had a car dealership in Canada call me up, wanting to put together a jingle. I was so excited about making some cash, I (stupidly) jumped right in and started to work on the project without seeing one penny. After turning in the initial draft of the jingle, the general manager indicated that what I created didn't hit the mark. So, I proceeded to make another version, and then another. This pattern went on for a few weeks. At some point, I woke up. It dawned on me that I was spending hours and hours on a project that wasn't going anywhere. Given how I was going about things, who do you think was assuming all of the risks? It was me! This car dealership never spent any money. As a result, it did not really feel the pressure to move the project in the right direction. In fact, I later realized this dealership was basically window shopping—not looking to actually make a purchase. If I had insisted on a deposit, this would have saved me weeks of wasted time.

When asking for deposits, some customers will give you a hard time, despite the previous recommendations made just a moment ago. When this happens, you still have another card to play: ask your client to send a postdated check.

Let's say your customer is apprehensive about sending you money before hearing results. Ask to be sent a check dated for two weeks out; prior to the fourteenth day, you promise to send the customer the first draft of the jingle. Upon your doing so and proving that you're capable, the customer should allow the check to be cashed at that time. Should you not demonstrate that you are up to the job—as evidenced by your initial draft—the customer is free to place a stop-payment on the check. When taking this path, don't lead the customer to believe it will hear perfection by the deadline. Rather, it should expect to hear the building blocks for a great music campaign. Sure, you'll be under a lot of pressure, but this is the time when you need to trust your musical instincts.

Be bold. Ask for the deposit.

If it works out, you've got cash and a little less financial pressure bearing down on you.

DON'T EVEN THINK ABOUT IT, BRO

Let's finish our discussion on the contract with one more thing—giving your agreement some *teeth*.

Most musicians have lost a little sleep over worrying whether someone will eventually steal a chart-topping song from them.

As you send music over to advertisers, who's to say they won't rip you off? The reality is, you can't stop someone from cheating you. However, you can present such severe potential consequences that the prospect of doing so loses its appeal.

In section 9, the contract makes it clear that stealing the work or using it outside the boundaries set will result in the customer's spending far more than it would by simply purchasing the service under the terms outlined. This, in essence, is the "teeth" I alluded to a moment ago. You want to make it abundantly clear that ripping you off is not a smart option; it will be a costly mistake.

Get with your attorney and craft language that spells out what should happen if your customer does not do all it agreed to.

18

HIRING OTHER MUSICIANS

Earlier in the book I talked about the need for you to establish your talent pool. As you grow your jingle business, there will come a time when you will be asked to provide musical content outside the scope of your capabilities; it may be vocals, a proficiency with a particular instrument, or a production-related skill. Whatever the case, you will find yourself at a point where you need to hire someone.

When I say "hire," I mean to pay someone to participate in one of your projects—not employing a guy to work forty hours a week for you. When you hire people on a per-project basis, these folks will be your contractors. You pay them for a service and they're done. In reality, they're like you—working for themselves—using their musical or technical skills.

When working with these people, abide by this rule: *If I'm getting paid, you're getting paid.*

There have been times when I reached out to singers to participate in a jingle project. In their excitement, some have volunteered to sing for free. I don't mind having people *audition* for free, but if a client of mine takes the version of the jingle that features a singer and pays me, I feel it is my obligation to pay the contributing musician, regardless of his or her pro bono offer. You may think, "Uh, not me, dude. I'll take as much money as I can get!" Trust me, I know what it means to be on the lookout for every extra penny. However, there are limits. Do not let your desire for a few extra bucks overshadow one of the most important resources you have—people! When I agree to pay singers or musicians, they are incredibly thankful and appreciative. As a result, these people put in their best work for me; they sing harder and play with more skill. Think about yourself for a minute; what would be the quality of your work at your regular job if your boss told you that your usual check will not be forthcoming? Uh, yeah, they'd have to call security because you'd go absolutely stupid-nuts right there in front of everybody, right? This perfectly illustrates that it's all about the Golden Rule, people! Start giving what you want to get. Besides, it's pretty empowering when you're the guy or gal sitting back cutting *other people's* checks. You start to feel like, well, a real business owner. Guess what? You are!

So, let's talk pay for your helpers.

One of the toughest roads you'll have to navigate with your contractors is how much to pay them. What is the going rate for a singer to lay down a few tracks or a guitarist to come in and jam out a sweet solo? Chances are, you won't come across any structured info on this unless you're a part of some type of union.

You see, in the upper echelons of creative industries, contractors join unions—actors unions, songwriter's unions, audio engineering unions, and so on. As a service to members, unions provide guidance on how much one should be paid for participating in a project, a.k.a. *scale*.

Having said all that, it is likely that the vast majority of you reading this book are not in a union, so I'll spare you the details of that rabbit trail and take you back to square one: how much to pay those helping you?

I think it's a pretty solid strategy to pay people based on the size of your jingle contract. If I'm working on a pretty small project, my singers will be paid a small amount. If the project is big, I'd pay them much more. To make things more uniform and consistent, you could even opt to pay them a percentage of the total package price agreed upon with your client.

I feel a good percentage to offer major participants is 5 percent.

Major participants will be those featured in a clear, obvious way. For instance, a lead vocalist is always a major participant in my book. There are times when an instrumentalist can take on this role. Let's say your customer requests a skilled banjoist. I might decide to pay this instrumentalist a major-participant wage due to the specialized skill he or she brings to the table.

Given the many facets of music, there could even be times when you have multiple major participants in one jingle.

Don't worry about the loss of money when paying multiple people. If you follow the advice outlined in the "What to Charge" chapter, you will price your jingles in such a way to account for projects that are more involved, i.e. needing more participants.

So, if you go with my 5 percent recommendation, this is how pay will work out for your contractors:

Total Jingle Revenue	Talent Payout
$2000	$100
$3500	$175
$5000	$250

Should you follow my payout model for hiring people, know that there will be some who will be insulted by how *little* you are willing to pay. On the opposite side of the spectrum will be others who are elated by the money they can earn with you. The point being, it's an open market. The cumulative reaction you receive from real musicians you are looking to hire will inform whether your payout model is reasonable.

Just be careful that you don't get "guilted" into overpaying for the help of musicians. They, and you, need to be mindful that *you* spent time and money on this book. *You* had to learn the business. *You* hunted for customers. *You* built the website and on and on. Therefore, *you* should be earning far more than any of your participants, as you are the business owner.

Welcome to capitalism!

19

THE BONUS ROUND

As I get ready to wrap up and send you off into the world to make some cash producing jingles, I'd like to share a few insider secrets that will give you a definite edge.

Welcome to the bonus round!

Do It Free

This entire book has been about making money with music, but now I'm telling you to make music for *nothing*? Am I going all contradictory on you again? No. Allow me to show you when making jingles for free may be advantageous.

As you're out there looking for clients, you will inevitably come across a business that is on the fence—it seems interested in what you do, but it is not ready to write any checks—it's just there . . . staring at you! If the business has not completely rejected you, it may be safe to assume your prices are not too crazy. You can also conclude that musical samples you sent were adequate enough to show that you've got skill. What the company may be struggling with, at this point, is whether you're capable of creating a sound that will be suitable for its specific business.

On rare occasions like this, I have taken the opportunity to create a *free*, custom jingle sample for the business. When I say "free," I don't mean let the client have it for free; I mean I create a customized jingle demo for that specific business without requiring an initial contract and 50 percent deposit. In the event that it doesn't like my work, the business can walk away and is not obligated to send me any payment. If, however, it sees promise in what I do, I then require that the company sign my contract and send a deposit, as we agree to continue to work on the jingle.

When you agree to create a free, customized jingle sample, you clearly shoulder all of the initial risk—a fact you should highlight with the business you're dealing with. The point of this exercise is to quickly build trust. In effect, you're saying, "Hey, I'm willing to stick my neck out to prove that my services are worth the investment."

As you consider this strategy, I'd caution you not to go around offering free jingle samples to everything that moves. Only offer this option when you feel you have a bona fide prospect or when you feel that the potential payoff is worth the risk and time.

Move Fast . . . Very Fast!

As I look back on my years in this business, there has always been something that has bothered me. To be truthful, this thing led me to losing some of my initial enthusiasm for the business and lots of money; it was *loss of customer engagement.*

Whenever I start a jingle for a client, everyone is happy, excited, and dialed in. The company is excited about hearing the first drafts for its jingle; I'm excited because I just pocketed a 50 percent deposit. Life is good. That is, unless the project drags on from one week to another, and another.

The process of recording a jingle may be prolonged for a number of reasons: the business owner decided to go on vacation, the guy you hired to sing for you lost his voice, the business you're working for has a major sales event and nobody has time to talk to you, and on and on.

No matter the reason, I've concluded that when a jingle project is not completed in the first two weeks of signing the contract, things can go bad quickly.

Structure your recording schedule and communications with your clients in such a way that you complete everything within two weeks of signing the contract.

If your process drags on for too long, you'll notice customers' picking apart every creative idea you have, or you may notice the business owner has drastically shifted his or her desires or likes and dislikes. There may even be instances when you're unable to get the business to respond to e-mails or phone calls; another possible indication of a souring business relationship.

So, what's the potential impact on your business?

If a customer loses interest for creating a jingle, it will become increasingly hard for you to create a sound it likes. The more ideas it rejects, the more likely it is to send you on a chase for perfection—a hunt for the elusive audio-unicorn. As a result, you won't be seeing the final payment for your jingle for some time.

I once agreed to make a jingle for a business in Anchorage, Alaska. When we started, everyone was totally excited. I had my down payment; the company had the anticipation of hearing something awesome. As we got started on the project, I sent over two or three initial ideas. However, I did not get prompt feedback from the client. As time went on, I stopped hearing from the firm altogether. You'd think that if a company is willing to drop over a grand on a deposit that it would at least want to communicate with the guy that took its money. Nope. After a few weeks of constant e-mails and phone calls, I finally learned that the lady I'd dealt with in the marketing department had left the company. *Whew.* There I was thinking that my jingles were being shunned. I'm in the clear, right? Again, no. It took forever for the new guy to be hired. Once he was on board, he had other pressing issues to deal with before he picked up where his predecessor had left off. And when he finally got around to reviewing my jingle ideas, I was instructed that everything I had created sucked and we needed to start afresh. After absorbing this debilitating blow and a ton of back-and-forth, I, to my discredit, wound up finishing this jingle project nearly *two years* later! I blame myself. It was absolutely preposterous and I never should have allowed it to go on that long! The completion terms of my contract should have been stronger and I should have recognized that moving quickly in the initial stages was critical.

In my studio, there's a whiteboard where I log all my expected income. Every month, I'd see the money I should have been enjoying from this customer but that I wasn't. It was a constant reminder that customer excitement has a short shelf-life.

Maintaining a high level of engagement and productivity in the first couple of weeks can mean the difference between getting half and all of your money. As a result, be sure your contract and your responsiveness to the recording process moves you to deliver within the first few weeks of your business relationship.

High Mileage

Selling jingles is a lot like selling a car—if made well, it can last for many years. That's an awesome takeaway for a business. However, this setup does not bode well for you, the jingle producer. Once you make your money from one customer, chances are that the business may not need you for a long time—or ever again.

One thing you can do to help yourself out is offer strategic updates.

For instance, you may opt to contact the business again and propose a Christmas version of the client's jingle—just in time for holiday advertising. Or you may offer other event/seasonal upgrades to the music.

The key to making this strategy work is charging a fraction of the original cost for subsequent renditions. So, let's say you originally charged $2,500 for a jingle package; you may offer to make a holiday version of the same jingle for $750.

The updated version of your jingle does not have to be a reinvention of the wheel. As for the Christmas update, it could be as simple as throwing in a few sleigh bells and carol-style vocals into the original mix.

Whatever you decide, make the revision/update worthwhile—both logically and financially.

Jingle-Sales Program

Earlier in the book I mentioned that you can reach out to radio, TV, and cable broadcasters to see whether they'd be willing to introduce you to their client base. I'd like to take you a step beyond that, to something even more lucrative—a jingle-sales program.

Sometimes referred to as jingle cattle calls, jingle-sales programs are big events stations put on to draw in as many local businesses as possible. These events are exclusively for advertisers and are usually held at a fancy hotel or some other high-end facility. Over the course of one to two days, businesses are invited in so the station's sales staff can wine and dine them. As you'd imagine, the number one objective is for the station to sell advertising space or airtime. To achieve this goal, stations have been known to bring in outside help. This is done to offer an incentive for these businesses to advertise. In this case, it would be your jingle services. When this happens, stations will actually pay you, the jingle producer, to work on behalf of the customers they are wooing. This act demonstrates that the stations are willing to invest in the success of their advertisers.

Here's an example of how this plays out: The owner of a local shoe store will be invited to the meeting by a radio station sales rep. When she arrives, she's offered food, pens, coffee mugs, and other collateral material. After the initial schmoozing, the meeting begins. A sales manager will get up and say a lot of great things about the station and why it is important to advertise with the station. The salesperson will also outline various advertising packages that can be beneficial for the visiting business. After this point—pause for dramatic effect—the jingle guy stands up. The station then tells the business owner that if she agrees to invest in one of the advertising packages, the station will throw in a jingle *for free*! Don't get nervous. Remember, the station has already struck a deal with you, the jingle company. Your service is free for the business owner. But behind the scenes, you're getting money directly from the station.

This whole setup is similar to upgrading to a new smartphone. Sure, the phone is free, but a contract is required. As you're paying your monthly phone bill, the phone company is paying the phone's manufacturer for the *free* device. And that, my friend, is the circle of life!

The beauty of jingle-sales programs is that they are like shooting fish in a barrel. A ton of advertisers show up for one event and you simply go after them.

One of my most successful jingle programs was held at a TV station in Orlando, Florida. The station flew me in and lined up over twenty of their best prospects for me to speak with. I conducted one-hour presentations to each business. I went in at seven a.m. and stayed in the conference room until the evening for two days. When it was all over, I had thousands of dollars in projects. All I had to do was fly back home and start recording them. Not bad for two days stuffed in a conference room.

Although I wouldn't advise this be your main strategy for selling jingles, you may try calling a few stations to see whether they'd give you a shot at conducting a jingle-sales program. Know, going into it, that this can be a tough road to travel, as a handful of large companies are already out there that already do this type of thing and have long-term contracts with many stations. You'll also come across a lot of salespeople who will tell you that buying jingles will exceed their budget or that they simply don't want the service.

Landing a jingle-sales program alliance with a station is incredibly rewarding. However, if you're going to succeed in doing so, you're going to need a lot of patience and have the willingness to keep knocking on doors until a station takes you seriously and gives you a chance.

Audio Exports

Throughout this book, you may have noticed a pattern. You might've picked up on my saying that I've created jingles in such places as Florida and Alaska, though I do not reside in these places. In fact, I've recorded material for customers in Canada, the United Kingdom, the Middle East, and South Africa.

One of the most important things you need to grasp is that the world is a huge place and you eventually need to pursue opportunities beyond where you live.

During the first few years making jingles around my town, things started to cool down a lot. I'd call the local radio and TV stations—I got no love. I tried reaching out to production houses and ad agencies in the city—still no interest. At some point, I concluded that things were pretty dead around town and that I needed to take my show on the road.

I'd send e-mails and make phone calls. With a bit of time and persistence, I started getting return phone calls and e-mail replies; things were beginning to happen—just elsewhere!

As you look for clients to buy your jingles, you're most likely going to stumble across some local dry patches from time to time. If that pattern seems to be never-ending, try calling similar businesses or stations in the next town over. From there, keep moving outward to other cities, states, or even countries. Eventually, you'll come across someone who wants what you have to offer. Given the global access the web provides, offering service for a customer halfway across the country is a nonissue.

The vast majority of work I've completed over the years has come from places nowhere near my home. You, too, can enjoy income from places beyond the edge of town. You just have to decide in your mind that it's an attainable objective.

20

IT'S YOUR TURN

Okay, when we started, it's possible you didn't anticipate just how much there is to this business. My hope is that the info shared will help you earn the money you deserve. Having said that, we've covered a lot of material; your head may be swimming in details. I don't want you stumbling away from this book with a lot of facts and no direction. As a result, I'd like to offer you an action plan to get you in business.

As we go through the recommended sequence of actions, I do so with the understanding that you already have things in place, such as your business name, website, jingle demo, contract and so on:

WEEK 1

1. E-mail or call 5 radio stations.
2. E-mail or call 3 local TV stations.

WEEK 2

1. E-mail or call 5 local full-service ad agencies.
2. E-mail or call 3 local production houses.

WEEK 3

1. E-mail or call 6 local businesses you've observed on air.
2. Send follow-up correspondence for those contacted in weeks 1 and 2.

WEEK 4

1. E-mail or call 10 radio/TV stations in a different city.
2. E-mail or call a large or midsize ad agency, no matter the location.
3. Send follow-up correspondence to businesses contacted in week 3.

After you're done with week 4, you'd start the process all over again, starting from week 1, adding new places to call as you come across those who reject your services or are unresponsive.

Ideally, the outlined weekly activities should not take much time—less than an hour. If you're not getting the results you want, opt to add more places to call. Know that finding your first deal is a numbers game—the more people you call, the more likely you are to strike gold.

Increase your odds of finding a customer by upping the number of people you call and e-mail.

Finally, you may feel that your day job will get in the way of calling or e-mailing people. Don't let that stop you. Use your breaks at work to your advantage. Grab your smartphone and escape to a quiet place and make a handful of calls. Initially you may not feel that you are accomplishing much, but all it takes is just *one* yes; you really never know which call will lead you down that path. Instead of wasting your lunch hour poking through pics on social media or hanging out with people who aren't ambitious, use this time to find some *jingle money*!

AFTERWORD
All Right, Let's Bring It In

I recently heard my pastor say something very simple, yet powerful. In essence, he said, "It's one thing to read a book about marriage, and it's another to actually be married while seeking to apply what you have learned by reading." This journey is no different. Now that you've gone through this book, the real magic happens when you actually get up and *apply* the concepts we've covered. Don't sit around thinking about it; make a decision to get out there and put this newfound knowledge to work. By going through this book, you have declared you want to make thousands writing jingles. Well, here's your chance. You've got the know-how to start!

As you begin your journey to making money, you're going to hear no along the way. But if you don't give up and stick to what we've covered, I've got a feeling I'll be hearing from you soon: I'll be listening for your work online, on TV, the radio, and beyond!

God bless,

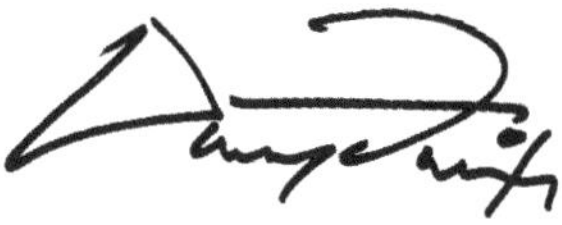

Walt

FREE RESOURCES

Although some good pay-to-play resources may prove to be useful for your selling jingles, I believe it will be helpful for you to start out by using some of these free tools:

Advertising Agency Directories

aaaa.org
adage.com

Broadcast Directories

allaccess.com
stationindex.com
tvnewsday.com

Find Businesses & People

zoominfo.com (search for FREE Community Edition)
linkedin.com
Google Maps (search for businesses, such as dentists, car dealers, etc.)

Places to List Your Company

jinglestop40.com
fmqb.com
rbr.com
rab.com
radiojinglespro.com
radio411.com
radiotoday.co.uk

Share/Feature Your Music

SoundCloud.com
YouTube.com
Vimeo.com

DropBox.com
Google Drive

E-mail Services

phpList.com
MailChimp.com
VerticalResponse.com

Brochures & Graphics

pixlr.com
canva.com
gimp.org
Google Docs

NOTES

WHY JINGLES ARE POWERFUL

1. David Huron, "Music in Advertising: An Analytic Paradigm," *Musical Quarterly* 73, no. 4 (1989), 557–74.
2. Peter Noel Murray, PhD, "Inside the Consumer Mind," *Psychology Today*, February 26, 2013, https://www.psychologytoday.com/blog/inside-the-consumer-mind.
3. Malini Mohana, *Music & How It Impacts Your Brain, Emotions*, PsychCentral.com, http://psychcentral.com/lib/music-how-it-impacts-your-brain-emotions/.

NO COPYING

1. http://www.copyright.gov/.

WHO WILL BUY YOUR JINGLES?

1. http://www.investopedia.com/terms/e/errors-omissions-insurance.asp.